Lost Restaurants

OF

FORT LAUDERDALE

Lost Restaurants
OF
FORT LAUDERDALE

TODD L. BOTHEL AND DAN SANTORO

AMERICAN PALATE

Published by American Palate
A Division of The History Press
Charleston, SC
www.historypress.com

Front Cover

Top left: Proprietor Donald "Porky" Baines at Porky's Hide Away, 1960s. *Courtesy of History of Fort Lauderdale.*

Top center: Lunch menu at the Bivans Hotel, 1925. *Courtesy of the Broward County Historical Archives, Broward County Library, Easter Lily Gates Collection.*

Top right: Johnny's Eldorado signage, 1970s. *Author's collection.*

Bottom: Looking north, across the New River, at the Pioneer House, 1970s. *Author's collection.*

Back Cover

Tale O' the Tiger menu cover, 1960s. *Courtesy of the* Fort Lauderdale News.

Brown's Good Food, located in the Bryan Arcade, circa 1936. *Courtesy of the Broward County Historical Archives, Broward County Library.*

First published 2020
Manufactured in the United States

ISBN 9781467144605

Library of Congress Control Number: 2020932102

For all of the restaurant entrepreneurs of Fort Lauderdale who have provided unique venues and dining experiences for over one hundred years. And to Todd's sister, Chief Master Sergeant Trish D. Almond, Washington State command chief (retired), who served thirty-one years in the military and made a mean pot of mac and cheese as a kid.

Contents

CONTENTS

Acknowledgements

No author can complete a book without the assistance of a plethora of resources and individuals. In the course of drafting this manuscript, we have received help from many people and organizations.

We have a special appreciation for Erin Purdy, curator of historical archives at the Broward County Historical Archives, Broward County Library. She granted us access to research information and historical photographs and fulfilled our digital image requests.

Britt Farley, the head of special collections and archives at the African American Research Library and Cultural Center, Broward County Library, also provided us with research materials.

The research files at History Fort Lauderdale (the Fort Lauderdale Historical Society) were also of benefit, and the society supplied digital photographs of some of the old restaurants. Additional historic photographs were obtained from the State Archives of Florida, Florida Memory.

The Broward County Library's holdings of Miller's and Polk's Fort Lauderdale city directories helped us generate a working list of restaurants. Newspapers.com was also an invaluable resource.

The conversations we had with individuals also provided us with some historical background and interesting stories. Todd L. Bothel would like to say a special thank-you to his coauthor, Dan Santoro, for conducting most of these interviews. The individuals interviewed for this book included Sandra Chichester Blaikie, Cindy Sowers Burlingame, John Day, Darrell House, Jack Jackson, Mike Koch, Dean Middlebrooks, Ted Pizio,

Clint Ramsden, Frank "Butch" Samp, Scott Watson, Ginger Willis and Lawrence "Zero" Zimmerman.

Articles that have been written over the years by *Fort Lauderdale News*, *Fort Lauderdale Daily News* and *Sun-Sentinel* reporters and editors provided insight into the restaurant industry. These writers included Pat Brown (*Fort Lauderdale News* nightclub columnist), Dick Hoekstra (*Fort Lauderdale News and Sun-Sentinel* amusement editor), Robert Tolf (*Sun-Sentinel* and *Florida Trend* restaurant reviewer), Randye Hoder (*Sun Sentinel* staff writer), Bob Freund (*Fort Lauderdale News* entertainment writer and editor) and Michael Mayo (*Sun-Sentinel* dining critic).

Our appreciation goes to Jacqueline Goldstein, curator of the Jewish Museum of Florida-FIU, for proofreading and editing the draft.

And finally, we would like to give a big shout out to all of the restaurateurs of Fort Lauderdale for all of their years providing great service and dining experiences to the town's locals and the tourists. They have always helped make Fort Lauderdale a great destination. Many of them, including Sam Harris, Fred Franke, Chris Wagner, Fred Wenner, Jimmy Fazio, Louise Flematti, Bea Morley, John Carlone, Bobby Van, Ron Morrison, John Day and Jack Jackson, have owned and operated multiple restaurants and have been actively involved in the Fort Lauderdale and Broward County Restaurant Associations and chamber of commerce. There are also a number of other restaurant owners and operators that, unfortunately, cannot be listed within this book. However, we would like to show our appreciation for all of the restaurateurs and restaurants, both large and small, who have sacrificed and strived for greatness over the last 120 years.

Introduction

Come unto me, all ye that labor in the stomach, and I will restore you.
—M. Boulanger, 1765, motto over door of first restaurant

Native Americans came to the southeast region of Florida around 12,000 BCE. At the time of the European incursion into the Florida peninsula (1513 CE and onward), the Tequesta tribe was living in the Fort Lauderdale area (and had been since the third century BCE). The remaining Tequesta were evacuated to Cuba by the Spanish when the British took control of Florida from Spain (1763). The first white settlers, the family of Surles and Frankee Lewis of South Carolina and, later, the Bahamas, arrived on the New River in 1789.

Around the time that Florida was ceded to the United States from Spain by the Adams-Onis Treaty (effective 1821), the Seminole tribe had migrated to South Florida, and the Lewises had moved to Miami. By 1826, William Cooley had arrived on the New River, and by 1836, fifty residents lived along the river. Following the Dade Massacre (December 1835) in central Florida and the Cooley Massacre (January 1836) at New River, the Second Seminole War began. A series of three forts were built in the area in 1838 and 1839. Following the end of the Seminole Wars (1858), no one resided in the Fort Lauderdale region until around 1870, when the John Brown family was recorded as living there in the 1870 U.S. census. In 1876, a house of refuge (a life-saving station for wrecked sailors) was constructed, and until

1891, a series of station keepers and their families, who lived along the beach, were the area's only residents.

Frank Stranahan arrived in 1893 to operate the overnight ferry camp and establish a trading post with the Seminoles. The Florida East Coast Railway was extended south, from West Palm Beach to Miami, and the first train arrived in Fort Lauderdale on February 22, 1896. This opened the area to further settlement and brought fruit and vegetable brokers and fishing and hunting parties into town. The local hotels (for example, the Bryan Hotel) provided dining facilities, and by 1908, H.D. Braddock was maintaining an ice cream and lunch stand in the area.

The city of Fort Lauderdale (Dade County) was incorporated on March 27, 1911, when 45 qualified voters (of the 143 inhabitants) saw the need for municipal services. The Florida Fruit Lands Company land auction was conducted by Richard Bolles, and it brought 3,000 land buyers to the area. This also most likely played a part in the town's incorporation. These new residents could purchase a piece of land in Progresso (North Fort

Oldest known image of an eatery in Fort Lauderdale. Located on Wall Street, 1909. *Courtesy of History Fort Lauderdale.*

Lauderdale) and an accompanying tract in the as-yet-undrained Everglades. This influx of people necessitated the new construction of mercantile stores, lumber yards, clothing stores and restaurants. In 1915, Broward County was formed from Dade County, and Fort Lauderdale became the county seat. That same year, the Dixie Highway was extended to Fort Lauderdale, allowing automobiles to travel to the city.

Over the next fifteen years, Fort Lauderdale saw dramatic growth. By 1920, the city's population totaled 2,065. In February 1925, the area's population was just 5,625, and it had grown to 15,315 by December of the same year. The town's early restaurants included the Blue Onion, Meyer's Café, Walsh's Restaurant, A.G. Restaurant, Glade Restaurant and the Green Room Restaurant. Most of these restaurants were located in the downtown area (Andrews and Brickell Avenues), and there was new growth along Las Olas Boulevard. The Las Olas Roof Restaurant, in the Bland and Driggers Building, opened to great fanfare on December 3, 1925. Unfortunately, it was one of many building casualties (along with 3,500 others) during the 1926 hurricane. Due to the destruction caused by the hurricane, Fort Lauderdale entered an era of economic depression three years before the rest of the country entered the Great Depression. The town's population had dropped by approximately half (8,668) by 1930.

During the 1930s, leading up to the start of World War II, Fort Lauderdale was a sleepy resort town. Restaurants would open for the winter season to serve northern visitors and then close again for the summer. However, by the end of the decade, the city was growing again (in the 1940 census, the population totaled 17,996). *Miller's Fort Lauderdale Florida City Directory* of 1938–39 stated in its preface, "The number of excellent eating places created and developed here has kept pace with the other growth of the city, and it is possible to procure as excellent prepared food under as pleasant surroundings as anywhere in the state and in a wide variety of places."

World War II brought an influx of U.S. Navy personnel (including George H.W. Bush) to Fort Lauderdale for training at the naval air station. The service men's center and the town's restaurants served many meals to these future "defenders of freedom." Some of the new restaurants that were opened during this time included the Chick House, the Dutch Mill, Davis Cafeteria and the Briny Deep.

After the war, many of these servicemen moved back to the area, and Fort Lauderdale saw a significant increase in its population size (in the 1950 census, the population totaled 36,328; in the 1960 census, the population totaled 83,648) and tourism rates. Just like the boom in the 1920s, more restaurants were needed to cater to the locals and tourists. The town's growth of restaurants took place along South Federal Highway and Andrews Avenue; the Sunrise Boulevard and Federal Highway corridor; North Federal Highway; and, eventually, along Oakland Park and Commercial Boulevards. As George Bacher stated in a September 1963 *Fort Lauderdale News* editorial, "Generally, vacationers and residents have found they receive a tremendous value in price and quality in the area's restaurants."

Live entertainment has always been a part of the restaurant experience in Fort Lauderdale. Starting in the 1930s, and through the 1940s and 1950s, performers from the north would come to town for the winter season. Local entertainers were also regular performers in the area's restaurants. The postwar era saw larger restaurants being constructed, and the 1960s and 1970s brought more nationally known acts (like Jerry Lee Lewis, the Spinners, Ray Charles, Louis Armstrong, Phyllis Diller and Tanya Tucker). Depending on the restaurant, one could hear jazz, easy listening, big band, pop or rock. This tradition continues today, with local musicians performing in many of the town's restaurants.

The early 1970s saw the town's departure from seasonal openings. Fort Lauderdale emerged as a year-round resort; it not only catered to tourists but also tried to keep pace with a growing local population that sought entertainment twelve months a year. According to Dean Middlebrooks, the late 1970s and early 1980s were very exciting times in the city, which rivaled Las Vegas of the same era. Jack Zink stated in a March 30, 1976 *Fort Lauderdale News* article, "The seventies brought a new era in entertainment and nightlife to Fort Lauderdale and Broward County. So strong has the activity become that, except during a few brief weeks at the height of the winter tourist season, the area eclipses glamorous Miami-Miami Beach as the pulse of the entertainment world on the Gold Coast." The restaurant industry has continued to grow in Fort Lauderdale since that time.

Today, Fort Lauderdale is a top tourist destination, attracting millions of visitors annually. Port Everglades is the third-busiest cruise port in the United States, and the Fort Lauderdale–Hollywood International Airport is the eighteenth-busiest airport in the country. Many of the town's visitors (and its 183,000 locals) make full use of the numerous and diverse restaurants within the city.

Over the last 120 years, Fort Lauderdale has seen thousands of restaurants come and go. This book presents just a smattering of these eateries. Not included in this selection were the restaurants that were located in the

Lonely restaurant building that survived the devastating downtown fire, 1912. *Courtesy of the Broward County Historical Archives, Broward County Library.*

numerous downtown and beachside hotels (like the Polynesian Room at the Yankee Clipper, the Nassau Room at the Escape Hotel, and Stouffer's Anacapri Inn and Restaurant and the Colonel's Table at the Governors' Club Hotel). The area's regional chains (including Lum's, Royal Castle, New England Oyster House and Taco Viva) were also not featured.

PART 1

IT'S A MATTER OF CULTURE

Every restaurant needs to have a point of view.
—Danny Meyer

Since the earliest days of modern settlement in Fort Lauderdale (the mid-1890s), there has always been a diverse mix of cultures in the area. The early white settlers (of many nationalities) were joined by Seminole natives, Bahamians and African Americans (who had come to construct the railroad tracks). All of these groups were present in the area when the first train arrived in 1896. The advent of the railroad brought more farmers from the North to the area; these farmers were a combination of European whites (English, Irish, German, Danish and Swedish) and African Americans. An enclave of Jewish people arrived in the area in the late 1910s, and the land boom of the 1910s and 1920s brought both white and black businessmen to the area. As the town's population grew, there was also a growing need for additional restaurants. Restaurants of all varieties and sizes sprang up around the area. In the late 1920s, the Palm Garden Café offered Hungarian goulash as a specialty. Chinese food arrived in this small southern town in the late 1930s.

The Seminoles remained on the edge of the growing town, with a camp at Sailboat Bend (Southwest Fourth Avenue) and the Tommie Village (101 Northwest Fifteenth Avenue). Though the Seminoles did not operate any restaurants, tourists probably ate some of their traditional foods when they stopped by the camps for souvenirs. The Seminoles were moved to the Dania Reservation in 1924.

Opened in the early 1940s, the Chick House was located at 1008 East Las Olas Boulevard. Advertisements promoted "southern fried chicken at its best" and the "best waffles you ever tasted." *Author's collection.*

A color line was established in 1922, relegating the African American community to the northwest section of Fort Lauderdale. Dining establishments were operating in that area before then; however, it wasn't until 1936 that black-owned businesses were listed in *Miller's Fort Lauderdale Florida City Directory*. Some of these—and later eateries in the area—included the Royal Palm Café, the Deep Sea Chop House, Osborn's Restaurant and Chester's Place.

The post–World War II era brought more people to Fort Lauderdale and saw the rise of many more ethnic restaurants; Italian, French, German, Chinese, Spanish and Southern eateries spread across the city. It wasn't until the late 1960s that Caribbean blacks and Hispanic people began to immigrate to the area in large numbers. Eventually, representatives from all of these ethnic groups entered the restaurant business. While many of these eateries have come and gone, some of them have achieved longevity; these success stories include the Mai Kai (Polynesian, opened in 1956), Henry's China House (opened in 1959), Don Arturo's (Cuban, opened in 1975) and Old Heidelberg (opened in 1991).

1
African American

BLUE FLAME BAR AND GRILL

The Blue Flame Bar and Grill was located at 422 Northwest Fifth Avenue and was a popular eating establishment in the 1950s and early 1960s. It was operated by Lucile and Johnnie Brewer, and people came from all over town to eat there. Johnnie allegedly ran an illegal gambling operation (he was arrested several times), but he became a civic leader in the northwest quadrant of town (the historic black community).

The Blue Flame Grill was a popular spot within the African American community, 1964. *Courtesy of History Fort Lauderdale.*

Both Lucile and Johnnie attended Dillard High School, and after they got married, they worked on a farm until they had enough money to open their eating establishment. In 1948, Johnnie received authorization to construct a store building at 422 Northwest Fifth Avenue. In 1949, he opened a sundries store before turning it into a poolroom. By 1950, it became known as Lucile Brewer's Lunchroom, and by 1956, the name had been changed to Blue Flame Bar and Grill. The restaurant's specialty was fish and grits. Patrons could catch a whiff of the meals that Lucile made for Johnnie, which included smothered pork chops and smothered liver. Lucille would add these dishes to the restaurant's menu at the request of customers.

The restaurant operated until 1964, when it fell victim to urban renewal. In the mid-1960s, large tracts of the historically black neighborhoods of Fort Lauderdale were leveled for new construction projects. Today, the site of the Blue Flame Bar and Grill is part of the Regal Trace apartment complex.

TASTY LUNCHEONETTE

The Tasty Luncheonette was located at 315A Northwest Fifth Avenue, in an area that was affectionately called "Short Fifth" in the African American section of Fort Lauderdale. Willie Freeman was the owner, and it was open from 1955 to 1973. Dr. James L. Bass, the first black dentist in Fort Lauderdale, had his office on the second floor of the building.

The Tasty Luncheonette in the historic African American section of Fort Lauderdale, with Dr. Bass's dentist office on the second floor, 1964. *Courtesy of History Fort Lauderdale.*

The Tasty Luncheonette was "where the pig became famous," and according to Florence Cohen, it was the "place for the best food on Fifth Avenue." She continued, "Willie was real professional looking and a wonderful cook. I don't know anybody who didn't eat there during those times." George Burrows Jr., whose father was the first licensed black electrician in Broward County, recalled that he and his father regularly frequented the Tasty Luncheonette. "I used to ride with him during the day, and we'd stop there for lunch. In fact, my parents met there."

In December 1958, the Tasty Luncheonette hosted the dinner for the negro city champs of the Florida State Yo-Yo Championships that were being held in Fort Lauderdale. From 1962 to 1967, the restaurant was featured in the annual *Green Book*, a traveler's guidebook for service places, hotels and restaurants that were friendly toward African Americans in segregated America. Today, the site is a parking lot.

2

Asian

GEORGE YOUNG'S CHOP SUEY RESTAURANT

George Young Nam came to Fort Lauderdale in 1938, after spending thirty-four years in the restaurant business in New York City. He started preparing Chinese food at Brady's Barbecue (later the Log Cabin). In 1939, he operated George Young's Chinese Chop Suey Parlor in the Deck Dining Room (on the northeast corner of Andrews Avenue and River Drive) before moving over to Club Alamo.

The Marquee Restaurant hired Mr. Young in 1940 to prepare Chinese dinners. By 1941, he was back at Club Alamo. He worked at Hebsacker's in 1942 before opening his own place, the Bamboo Bar and George Young's Chop Suey Restaurant, in 1943. Located at 222 Southeast Sixth Avenue (Federal Highway), George Young's only served Chinese fare. George operated the restaurant until 1947, when new ownership switched to Italian food.

George Young worked all over town, but for a short time, he had his own place. *Courtesy of the* Fort Lauderdale Daily News.

ASIA RESTAURANT

The short-lived Asia Restaurant was ideally located downtown, near the New River, but it was unable to remain in business. *Courtesy of the* Fort Lauderdale Daily News.

After opening in 1946, the Asia Restaurant was owned by Joe Jeff and located at 300 Southwest First (Brickell) Avenue. Jeff, a Chinese immigrant, moved to Fort Lauderdale in 1941 and operated Joe's Grocery and Market at 517 Northwest Fourth Street.

The Asia Restaurant served Chinese and American specialties. A 1946 newspaper article stated that the restaurant's two Chinese cooks turned out "chop suey, chow mein, moo goo cuy pan, yocker mein and chicken egg foo young" in an airy kitchen. Announcements by the Asia Restaurant in the restaurant section of the *Fort Lauderdale Daily News* during November and December 1948 declared, "Fort Lauderdale's only authentic Chinese restaurant. Chicken chow mein, tops! Also, American dishes. Flavorful food at its best. Orders to take out. Luncheon, 11–3; à la carte 3–5; dinner, 5–9."

The restaurant only remained open until 1950. Joe Jeff then opened the Cantonese Shop, which featured authentic Chinese art, goods and gifts. Today, the X Las Olas apartment and retail complex is under construction at the former Asia Restaurant site.

MOY'S CHINESE RESTAURANT

Around 1930, Jeanne Goon Moy and George Sing Moy emigrated from China to New York City. Jeanne's family had previously immigrated to Fall River, Massachusetts, in 1919 but had returned to China. During World War II, the Moys worked at Republic Machine Tool Corporation. On August 30, 1942, the family received a full-page spread, titled "A Chinese Mother Works for Uncle Sam," in the *New York Daily News*. In July 1944, Jeanne, the only Chinese woman in America who was a skilled machinist, was given the War Worker of the Week award.

The Moys also worked in restaurants, and most notably at the House of Chan (Seventh Avenue and Fifty-Second Street in Manhattan, New York). In 1946, at the urging of their friends Jerry and Lena Margro, the Moys began their seasonal commutes to South Florida with the goal of becoming restaurant owners. Following the flood of tourists, they purchased the Blue Plate Special Restaurant in Hollywood and converted it into a Chinese eatery. For the next several years, they returned to New York City during the spring and summer to earn money for supplies for the next winter season in Florida.

MOY'S

CHINESE RESTAURANT

"Authentic Chinese Food"

FREE

CHOP STICKS

WE TEACH YOU HOW
TO USE THEM
11:30 A. M. to 11:00 P. M.
321 S. Andrews Ave.
Phone JA 3-6748
Free Parking After 5 P. M.
Pigeon Hole Parking

Advertisement highlighting free chop sticks and lessons, 1959. *Courtesy of the Fort Lauderdale News.*

After establishing Moy's Chinese American Restaurant in Hollywood, the Moys opened the Golden Dragon in Miami Beach on December 14, 1950; it was bankrupt by May 1952. The Moys tried expanding again in 1954, when they opened a Moy's in Fort Lauderdale. It was located at 321 South Andrews Avenue and offered the same Cantonese dishes and exotic cocktails as the Hollywood location. The Fort Lauderdale location remained open until 1961; after it closed, the Moys concentrated solely on their Hollywood location. The Moys sold the Hollywood restaurant in 1973, after George died. In addition to owning and operating the Moy's Chinese American Restaurants, the Moys had been founders of the American Bank of Hollywood, where George had been a director. The Moys' old Fort Lauderdale location is now a parking garage.

MOY LEE CHINESE RESTAURANT

Winston and Moy Lee were both born in China and immigrated to the United States in 1936 and 1937, respectively. Winston cooked in several San Francisco hotels before moving to New York City in the early 1940s. The first restaurant he operated was the New Star in Brooklyn. Moy (born Ming Q. Wong, Ngun Moy Hum, according to her immigration papers) moved to America with her first husband, Wae Yin Tom, and ran several laundries in

The Lee Family toasts the New Year (4670, the Year of the Rat) at their restaurant. *Courtesy of the* Sun-Sentinel.

New York City. She left him in 1952 and turned to driving a taxi and making illegal alcohol to make ends meet.

Winston and Moy met in 1953; they were later married and opened the Sunrise Restaurant in Brooklyn. They operated several other Chinese restaurants in Manhattan and on Long Island. They moved to Miami Beach in 1962 and opened the House of Moy Lee. The restaurant became very popular, and in 1975, the Lees moved to Wilton Manors and opened the Moy Lee Chinese Restaurant at 2321 North Federal Highway, in the former Polly Davis Beefseekers' Inn. Three hundred people attended the restaurant's opening on January 27, 1975, including Fort Lauderdale mayor Virginia Young, who declared that it was "the best Chinese food [she'd] ever tasted." The 330-seat facility had a touch of elegance everywhere; the color scheme was a blend of reds, greens, blues and golds. However, in the hullabaloo of preparing for the grand opening, the Lees forgot to get a liquor license; Moy Lee's went its first tourist season without being able to serve drinks.

The restaurant served Cantonese, Mandarin and Szechuan cuisine, along with the Lees' brand of Brooklyn Chinese food, which included Chinsese dishes tailored to an American palate. The portions were large, and the ingredients were high quality and fresh. Moy Lee's would cook food any way its customers wanted it, and if their favorite dish was not on the menu, all they had to do was ask for it. The restaurant drew many famous patrons, including Jackie Gleason, Milton Berle, Jackie Mason, Brenda Lee and Greg Louganis.

In 1977, the Lees sold the Miami Beach location to concentrate their energy on the Fort Lauderdale restaurant. Moy Lee's hosted the first Miss Asian American Beauty Pageant on March 2, 1985. A Hawaiian Luau Show was added as entertainment in 1986. The House of Moy Lee restaurants made the Lees multi-millionaires, but in 1988, the restaurant was closed. Winston passed in 1990, and Moy lived until 2012. The building was demolished around 1993. Today, a Starbucks location occupies the site.

TEAHOUSE OF THE TOKYO MOON

Constructed in 1964 and located at 425 Seabreeze Avenue, the Teahouse of the Tokyo Moon was the brainchild of Loflin W. Smalley. Consisting of three levels, with an entrance over a Japanese garden bridge, the restaurant could seat over four hundred guests. An architect was not utilized; the building was assembled from the "vision" in Smalley's head.

Loflin Smalley left his Georgia farm with $7.50 in his pocket and moved to Fort Lauderdale in 1926. He was hired as a busboy at the Broward Hotel on Andrews Avenue (today Bubier Park), and within three years, he was made the hotel manager. As a side job, he started a car rental business. This business flourished, and in 1960, he sold his portion to Hertz. With an interest in Polynesian and Oriental culture, his residence on Navarro Isle, Kona Kottage, was built with those themes in mind.

In 1965, Smalley opened the Teahouse of the Tokyo Moon, which also had Polynesian and Oriental themes. On the first floor, the entranceway led to an open-air patio and an indoor dining room. The second- and third-level decks seated 150 and 100 guests, respectively. An enchanting waterfall of red, blue, yellow and green was set amid an environment of flowers and coral rock. Next to the main grill, there was a small boiling volcano for the customers who wanted a "volcano-broiled" steak. The restaurant featured a combination of Polynesian, Oriental and American foods. For more intimate dining, there was the Geisha House on the third floor, where 24 patrons could sit on pillows around several low tables. The Teahouse of the Tokyo Moon offered exquisite views of Sun Moon

Patio dining at the Teahouse of the Tokyo Moon. *Author's collection.*

Bay, the Intracoastal Waterway and Idlewyld to the west and the Atlantic Ocean to the east. Docks were constructed on the Intracoastal side of the restaurant to attract boat owners.

One unique experience offered by the restaurant was an exclusive island cruise aboard the *Queen of Venice*. The day and evening cruises would traverse the Nurmi Isles, in view of some of the town's most beautiful waterfront homes, before ending at Kona Kottage (Smalley's estate) for a private tour of its Oriental gardens.

The restaurant was very popular and hosted many civic events and private parties. A costumed dinner was once hosted at the restaurant by Mr. and Mrs. William Maurer; at the party, one guest, Mrs. Emerson (Mary) Buckley, was in the Madame Butterfly costume that she had worn on stage at the New York Metropolitan Opera. In a letter to the editor of the *Fort Lauderdale News* on February 17, 1965, Mrs. Cyril Cross of Piedmont, California, wrote:

> *They're Beautiful. I am a visitor from Piedmont, Calif., and have traveled extensively. In my travels I have never seen anything as beautiful as the Kona Kottage and the Tea House of the Tokyo Moon.*

On January 7, 1967, Loflin Smalley was killed by an unknown assailant. Mrs. Smalley kept the restaurant going until August 1970. Terry Kramer and George Clark bought the restaurant and renamed it the Islander Beef and Grog. It remained open until early 1975. The building was demolished in April 1978. Today, the restaurant Coconuts is located at the site.

3
Cajun

LAGNIAPPE CAJUN HOUSE

In 1983, Ron Morrison and David Rea partnered to open Lagniappe Cajun House at 230 East Las Olas Boulevard. The restaurant featured Louisiana-style (Cajun and Creole) cooking, even though Morrison was of Scottish descent and Rea was from Pennsylvania. The menu included blackened redfish, crawfish pie, gumbo, red beans and rice, jambalaya, muffalettas, Po Boys and andouille. Jazz music, which was usually performed live, accentuated the experience. As Robert Tolf of the *Fort Lauderdale News and Sun-Sentinel* stated in a 1983 article, "What a perfect way to begin a weekend… enjoying the immediate transport to another place, another culture, brought to life in the large dining room, with its courtyard atmosphere, its judicious blending of brick and wood, with second-story balcony windows bringing in the light, with eye-pleasing greenery planted here and there."

Beginning in 1984, Lagniappe Cajun House sponsored an annual Cajun festival on Las Olas Boulevard. There were seven thousand attendees at the fifth annual festival (1988). One of the patrons, Bob Savard, commented, "I loved it and the food with a passion." The restaurant received Critic's Choice Awards (second place in 1984 and first place in 1985) from *Travelhost* magazine. In 1988, Lagniappe Cajun House was forced to move when a new twenty-one-story skyscraper was built by the Stiles Corporation on the site.

The restaurant's new location at 200 West Broward Boulevard (100 block of Southwest Second Avenue) was a former warehouse and home to Auntie Mame's and, later, the Backstreet Bar. The space allowed diners to sit in

Ron Morrison, owner of Lagniappe Cajun House, marking the last day at the original Las Olas Boulevard location, 1988. *Courtesy of the* Sun-Sentinel.

booths on the main floor and listen to live jazz music and sample Cajun and Creole cuisine. A courtyard area with a pool featured rockabilly and zydeco (bayou jazz) bands. As Stephanie McLane mentioned on Facebook, it had "great food and ambiance." She continued, "Many of my friends visiting from Europe loved dining there." Unfortunately, this home was short-lived, as Lagniappe's closed in 1990.

Ron Morrison went on to own four other restaurants—Mistral, Evangeline, Sage and Reed's River House—before taking over the food operations at the Riverside Hotel in 1995. Mistral and Evangeline were part of the beach renovation project to take it from a college spring break scene to a more upscale tourist setting. David Rea opened the Olde Towne Chop House on the corner of Southwest Second Avenue and Southwest Second Street before selling his interest in 1995 and moving to Orlando. Today, the original site of Lagniappe Cajun House is home to the Fifth Third Bank Building and the second location now houses Stache Drinking Den + Coffee Bar.

Cuban and Spanish

EL CUBANO

El Cubano was a Spanish and American cuisine restaurant opened by C.L. Kelton and Joe A. Medina on December 13, 1947. It was located at 706 North Federal Highway and offered something new and different: "Food with a flavor." The restaurant had seating for fifty and offered drive-in and carhop services. Joe Medina was a member of the North Federal Business Men's Association and the North Lauderdale Improvement Association. The El Cubano served as the regular meeting place for the Fort Lauderdale Junior Chamber of Commerce.

Advertisement for the El Cubano, 1947. *Courtesy of the* Fort Lauderdale Daily News.

Partnership difficulties resulted in the sale and closing of the El Cubano in November 1950. Even though it was only open for a short time, it was well liked. A notice in the personal announcements section of the *Fort Lauderdale Daily News* from the week of May 12–19, 1948, declared, "DEAR JANE: I am going to let you in on a secret. Margie Medina is doing some real good American cooking at the El Cubano Restaurant, 706 N. Federal Highway. Sincerely Mary. P.S. Almost forgot to tell you to do try their delicious Cuban sandwiches."

The Jalisco Mexican and Spanish Restaurant is located at the site today.

PANCHO'S CANTINA

Pancho's Cantina and Mexican Restaurant advertisement, September 21, 1984. *Courtesy of the* Fort Lauderdale News and Sun-Sentinel.

Located in the former Bushwackers, at 2428 East Commercial Boulevard, Pancho's Cantina opened in November 1983. It was launched by a partnership group comprised of Paul Proffer (Chuck's Steak House), John Day (Coconuts) and James Punter and Bill Brunberg (Bushwackers). The partners selected the name after putting the letters of their names into a hat and pulling out seven letters.

Pancho's had a large lounge with tile-topped stucco dividers. The walls were decorated with woven serapes and photographs of war scenes, banditos and old-time events. They served Mexican pizza, taco salad, quesadillas, chalupas, soft tacos, the Banana Burro and deep-fried ice cream. According to patrons, Pancho's also had very good guacamole.

However, Pancho's Cantina was short-lived. On October 9, 1985, it was reopened as Chuck's Steak House, which remains today. The lounge in Chuck's retains the Pancho's name.

Floribbean

MANGO'S

After the Sea Horse restaurant at 904 East Las Olas Boulevard closed in 1980, John "Jack" and Janet Boyle bought its building. They reopened the restaurant as Poet's in 1981. Both tourists and locals, especially the downtown lawyers, politicians and journalists, frequented the restaurant. Local legend has it that the letters of the name secretly meant "Piss on everything, tomorrow's Saturday!"

A frequent entertainer at Poet's was a young guitarist named John Day. He had arrived in Fort Lauderdale in 1969 aboard the forty-eight-foot sailboat *Valkyri*. Day found a steady flow of local gigs throughout the 1970s, including a gig at Chuck's Steak House on East Commercial Boulevard. Paul Proffer, the owner of Chuck's, offered Day part ownership in his new eatery, Friends Lounge at 2671 East Oakland Park Boulevard. A fast learner, by 1979, Day had partnered with Gene Merola at Bojangles (4000 North Federal Highway), and in the early 1980s, he opened Mango's in Marsh Harbour, Central Abaco, Bahamas. Day continued to play at Poet's and Coconuts, after it opened in 1981. Jack Boyle asked him to become a partner in Coconuts in 1986, and Day helped him build it into one of the most popular dockside restaurants in all of South Florida.

Poet's closed on August 1, 1992. The Boyles sold their controlling interest to Day and his partners. Day renovated and reopened the restaurant in late 1992 as Mango's. In a 2019 interview, Day stated, "I always liked tropical-themed, island-type restaurants, and, so, I decided to name the Las Olas store Mango's after my Bahamian place. So, we freshened the place up, put a lot of seafood appetizers and dinners on the menu and opened up the dance floor." Mango's featured indoor and outdoor (patio café) seating that could accommodate nearly three hundred people. It had an open-air Caribbean flair with cane bar chairs, a large bar and a band and dance area. Mango's was long known for casual food, free-flowing drinks and live bands on the weekends. One smash recipe on the menu was a salmon glazed in honey barbecue sauce that Day had eaten as a child in North Carolina. "I got a lot of strange looks from my chefs when I brought that in back in the 1990s," he laughed, adding, "But it became a great lunch item, one of our top sellers."

A proposed purchase of the restaurant by Big Three Restaurants Inc. of Orlando in 2013 fell through. However, the land that Mango's sat on was sold to the local Restaurant People Corporation. A deal for the restaurant could not be completed. In 2016, Day and his partners sold Mango's to a new group of owners led by Bruno Vaccari. Mango's (the first version) closed in January 2017. "We had a sweet offer and a great run, so it was time," Day

Owner John Day in front of Mango's, 1993. *Courtesy of the* Sun-Sentinel.

said. Mango's underwent a yearlong renovation that turned it into a glitzy and trendy South Beach–style nightclub and Italian restaurant. It reopened in February 2018 with American fusion cuisine. The new Mango's featured a design that was chicer and more modernist than the rustic and relaxed vibe of the original. The new look and menu were jarring to many longtime patrons. The whole venture was not well received. By June 2018, Mango's (the second version) had closed its doors.

Frank Talerico became the new owner of the building, and in February 2019, he opened Piazza Italia at the site. "Mango's, at one time, it was a nice spot, but it's had its day," Talerico said. "After two different owners and two closings, we figure we're better off starting over and going in a new direction."

CAFÉ BLUE FISH

Café Blue Fish was located at 3134 Northeast Ninth Street in the Sunrise (or North Beach) Village area of Fort Lauderdale Beach. The building is the former home of the Bamboo Shack (1953–62), Roberto's Italian American Restaurant (1967), Le Café du Beaujolais (1970–86) and Salty Sally's (1987–91). Café Blue Fish billed itself as "a little bit of Key West in Broward County," and for twenty years, it was true to its word.

As the *Sun-Sentinel* noted in its restaurant listing descriptions:

> *Café Bluefish is a quintessential Key West–style bar and restaurant that serves an array of tropical drinks and Floribbean fare. The chicken wings are meaty and delicious, and there's plenty of seafood, salads and burgers from which to choose. The drink list features rumrunners, daiquiris and margaritas, while draft beers are served in twenty-ounce mugs. The room opens to the street, so you can soak up the ocean air over breakfast, lunch or dinner.*

Longtime friends Paul Lorenzo, Frank "Butch" Samp and Chuck Feltman took over the building's lease in late 1991 and set out to create a relaxed, open-air restaurant that specialized in seafood and Caribbean snacks. Situated within a few steps of the Parrot, Banana Joe's and Primanti Brothers Pizza Grill, the area was a great place to bar and restaurant hop. After a few years, Lorenzo and Samp wanted to concentrate on their other restaurants and sold their shares to Feltman. He assembled a great staff—both in the kitchen

Popular bartender "Cooper" during the closing weekend of Café Blue Fish, 2012. *Author's collection.*

and in the front of the house—and the restaurant became a favorite of locals and tourists year-round.

"We were almost always busy," claimed ten-year manager and bartender Cindy Burlingame. "We had a great location, a good breeze off the ocean and a very good staff of popular bartenders and waiters. And the three different kinds of chicken wings and our seafood menu were hits also!" Almost everything on the menu was good. The lobster bisque and the tomato-based conch chowder were excellent, while the grouper and mahi-mahi sandwiches were fresh off the boat each day. The JuJu Hot and Jamaican jerked wings platters were not for the faint of heart. The fish wrap special, with a mango-pineapple salsa, was always worth a try. "One of our most popular bartenders was 'Cooper,' who would get his regulars to try different items off the menu so he could get a taste of them....He paid them back in beer and drinks," Burlingame recalled.

Café Blue Fish closed in May 2012, following a rent increase. Feltman threw a three-day closing bash with free food; the place was mobbed. Red Dog Cantina Tacos and Tequila opened at the location in July 2012 but only lasted for about a year. Today, the building still stands but is currently unoccupied.

6

French

LE CAFÉ DE PARIS

Opened in November 1961, Le Café de Paris was a mainstay on Las Olas Boulevard for nearly fifty-five years. Originally located at 701 East Las Olas Boulevard, Le Bistro de Paris (as it was first called) was opened by Andre Fredy. A third-generation chef, Fredy, who was of French descent, was born in Algiers, North Africa. He learned his trade at the Culinary Institute of Switzerland and the University of Culinary Arts in France. Interestingly, Fredy had served in the U.S. Army's Fifth Counterintelligence Corps during World War II.

Fredy moved to Broward County in 1961 (his parents were living here), and shortly after, he opened Le Bistro de Paris. His Parisian restaurant was a big success, and in 1962, he moved the restaurant a few doors to the east, at 715 East Las Olas Boulevard. There, Fredy created an intimate dining room that was truly of continental style and spirit. It was the place for the fashionable ladies and power brokers of Fort Lauderdale to meet over classics, like escargot bourguignon, beef Wellington and duck l'orange. After selling the restaurant, Fredy remained a chef and worked at various places, including the Playboy Club in Miami and Holy Cross Hospital, before opening Andre's in Pompano Beach (1980).

In the early 1960s, Louis Flematti immigrated to the United States. A Swiss native, he had graduated from a hotel and restaurant school in Switzerland and had always known that he wanted to work with food, wine and people. Flematti worked at New York's Waldorf Astoria Hotel and the Four Seasons Restaurant, but he moved to Florida because the New York winters were too cold. Once in Florida, he was hired at Le Dôme, where Fredy's father was on staff. In 1968, Flematti was hired as a waiter at Le Café de Paris (it had changed its name by then). The following year, he and a friend bought the restaurant from Fredy. Flematti received some of his backing from William Maus, the founder of the Maus & Hoffman store. By 1970, he was the sole owner.

Flematti and his French-born wife, Janine, spent the next forty-five years turning Le Café de Paris into a destination for classical French cuisine with an old-world ambiance. The two-story building had three intimate interior dining areas that were filled with antiques and an outdoor café space. Live entertainment was provided by a pianist (Patrician Zanghi since 1990). The restaurant's extensive menu included filet mignon béarnaise, lyonnaise potatoes, grilled lamb chops, onion soup, savory crepes and bottles of wine that cost up to $1,000. Phyllis C. commented on Tripadvisor's website, "Every time I go, I feel as if I'm just a few steps off of the Champ-Élysées! It's charming, rustic and romantic. The food is outrageous, and their wine list is outstanding. It has been one of my go-to special occasion restaurants for years and continues to be one of my favorites." Dave M. concurs, saying,

Le Café de Paris owner, Louis Flematti, preparing to retire and close the restaurant after more than fifty years in business in 2016. *Courtesy of the* Sun-Sentinel.

"A delicious and romantic dinner. The piano playing created a perfect atmosphere. The chicken cordon bleu was extraordinary. The bananas foster is unbelievably great. The staff oozes with pride and makes this a place you must visit." Flematti treated his staff like family and provided them with meals before their lunch and dinner shifts.

Recognized as Broward County's premier authentic French restaurant, Le Café de Paris garnered accolades from *Zagat Survey*, *Mobil Road Guide* and was a winner of a *Florida Trend* Award. The restaurant was so successful over the years that Mr. Flematti was able to buy property on and around Las Olas Boulevard. In 1986, he opened a second French restaurant, the French Quarter, around the corner from Le Café de Paris. Le Café de Paris closed on May 15, 2016.

LE DÔME OF THE FOUR SEASONS

In 1962, Nashville, Tennessee industrialist and financier Calvin Houghland purchased the Four Seasons cooperative apartment building at 333 Sunset Drive. An original unit owner in the building (which was constructed in 1958), Houghland converted it into Fort Lauderdale's first condominium residence in 1964. As a part of this transformation, Houghland renovated the top floor into the French restaurant Le Dôme. There, he created an elegant dining experience that featured *la haute cuisine*, the classic French style of preparing food, and French service, in which food was prepared at the guest's table. Chef Robert Morency, who formerly worked at Maxim's in Paris, was enlisted to work at Houghland's restaurant. Le Dôme also delivered dinner to the tenants in the building. Operating with a different menu every night for most of the month, Le Dôme's entrées were masterpieces of culinary art.

After opening on January 25, 1964, Le Dôme consisted of two dining rooms and two cocktail lounges, each with its own individual décor. Distinctive leaded and stained glass was added throughout the spaces, in addition to plush red carpet, period furniture, crystal chandeliers and original paintings on the wall. The restaurant could accommodate 160 diners, who were graced with magnificent 360-degree views of the city. The restaurant's ambiance was enhanced by its service and the personal attention of its expertly trained staff members in their tricolored uniforms and white gloves.

Le Dôme was honored by the Grand Council of *La Confrérie de la Chaîne des Rôtisseurs* (Guild of Meat Roasters) of Paris, France, in 1965, and it

Sketch of the proposed main dining room of Le Dôme on the eleventh floor of the Four Seasons Apartment Building, 1963. *Courtesy of the* Fort Lauderdale News and Sun-Sentinel.

received an award for "superlative achievement in interior design" from *Institutions Magazine* in 1966. For nine straight years (1967–75), the restaurant was bestowed with a five-star *Mobil Guide* Award (generally, the only South Florida restaurant to receive the reward).

In 1975, Le Dôme was sold to John Carlone, a former restaurateur of the Brave Bull Steak House, La Corrida and the Sea Watch. Significant changes occurred afterward, as Carlone began utilizing print media advertising (Houghland had spent little on this), expanded the menu beyond French food (instituted "Europe for Two" dinners) and began offering early bird specials. He wanted to move away from the older, wealthier clientele of seasonal snowbirds, to a more predominately local crowd. These changes led to an influx of customers; the restaurant went from serving 100 to 125 meals on weekdays and 175 meals on weekends to 225 on weekdays and 400 on weekends.

Doug Mackle bought Le Dôme in 1988. He was a graduate of the Florida International University School of Hotel, Food and Travel Services, and he was a former co-owner of Takeyama and Mackle Japanese Restaurant. He was also the owner and manager of Shirttail Charlie's when it opened in 1984. Mackle introduced a theater ticket and dinner package that was very successful. Le Dôme received several *Florida Trend Magazine* Golden Spoon Awards. In June 1996, Mackle closed the restaurant. The penthouse floor was purchased by then–Nova Southeastern University president Ray Ferrero Jr., who remodeled it into a three-bedroom apartment.

LE CAFÉ DU BEAUJOLAIS

Incorporated in December 1969, Le Café du Beaujolais was operated by the three Teboul brothers (Leon, Guy and Richard). Originally from Dinard, France, a coastal town between Brittany and Normandy, the brothers had worked in their father's restaurant in Paris. Located at 3134 Northeast Ninth Street, at the former site of the Bamboo Shack (1953–62), Le Café du Beaujolais was a small place, dripping with Gallic flavor. The building featured high ceilings, with red tones, impressionist art on the walls and chandeliers topped with small French shades. An excellent selection of French music played in the background, and during the 1970s, its menu included filet de sole belle meunière, langouste grillée à l'estragon, boeuf bourguignon, Chateaubriand, moules farcies and crevettes provençales. In "Tips on Tables" (*Fort Lauderdale News*, April 28, 1972), Ben Schneider declared the restaurant's escalope de veau à la crème as "sensational."

In 1978, Leon took sole control of the restaurant, as his two brothers had moved on to open La Reserve on Oakland Park Boulevard (now Bokamper's Sports Bar and Grill). Leon and his wife, Gisele (the sister of Andre Fredy, the original owner of Le Café de Paris), completely renovated the restaurant in 1980, expanding to the second floor of the building and assembling a twenty-thousand-bottle wine cellar. Advertisements from 1983 promoted the restaurant's exquisite classic French haute cuisine. Le Café du Beaujolais received *Florida Trend* magazine's Golden Spoon Award and *Wine Spectator*'s Best Wine List Award in 1984, 1985 and 1986.

Le Café du Beaujolais closed in 1986. Leon Teboul continued to own and operate La Reserve, Napoleon's Restaurant and Ginger's, and he was planning to open Leon's in Pompano Beach. After housing Salty Sally's for a few years, Le Café du Beaujolais's space became Café Blue Fish in 1991.

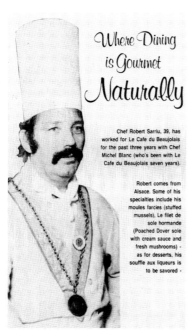

Where Dining is Gourmet

Naturally

Chef Robert Sarriu, 39, has worked for Le Cafe du Beaujolais for the past three years with Chef Michel Blanc (who's been with Le Cafe du Beaujolais seven years).

Robert comes from Alsace. Some of his specialties include his moules farcies (stuffed mussels), Le filet de sole hormande (Poached Dover sole with cream sauce and fresh mushrooms) - as desserts, his souffle aux liqueurs is to be savored -

Advertisement touting the specialties of Chef Robert Sarriu, 1978. *Courtesy of the* Fort Lauderdale News.

EDUARDO'S

Twenty Four Hundred Eduardo's was opened on December 10, 1970, at 2400 East Las Olas Boulevard by Eduardo di Sano. The restaurant featured an East Side New York look and a New Orleans–French menu. It replaced La Scala, which had moved to Pompano Beach. Before it became the home of Twenty Four Hundred-Eduardo's, the site had been the Terrace Patio Restaurant and Cocktail Lounge (1942–67). Di Sano had extensive experience as a restaurateur, having been involved with the Hasta Manaña (Coral Gables, Florida), the Court of the Shadows (North Miami), the Rose Room (San Mateo, California) and Eduardo's (Sherman Oaks, California). His Miami restaurants were favorites of presidents John F. Kennedy and Richard Nixon. He was joined in the operation by Chef Hill and his wife, Aimee di Sano.

The 225-seat facility was open for lunch, and dinner service was available in both the dining room and lounge. The house specialties included crabmeat remick a la pontchartrain and bananas foster. Live entertainment was provided, and on occasion, di Sano would "tinkle the ivories," as he had been a professional pianist in the 1930s. In 1974, di Sano sold Twenty Four Hundred Eduardo's to a group headed by James Colosimo. At that time, the restaurant's name was shortened to just Eduardo's, and it began operating all year long. It featured a romantic dining patio, with fountains, banyan trees, blue water pools, original Biagio Pinto paintings and evening entertainment.

Ciro Gentile became the owner of the restaurant in 1978, and he ran the operation as the maître d'. He had been a successful restaurateur on Long Island. At that time, Eduardo's began serving Italian cuisine. Ciro only

Opening week advertisement for the new Twenty-Four Hundred Eduardo's, 1970. *Courtesy of the* Fort Lauderdale News.

stayed at the restaurant for one year before selling out to Murray Krulik and taking over La Scala. During this time, food critics remarked, "Eduardo's provides one of the best dining experiences in the South," and they said, "[It] has become one of the best restaurants in town.'

Krulik owned the restaurant until 1984, when he sold it to Elio and Armando Orsini, Italian counts who owned Orsini's in New York. By October 1986, Orsini's was in chapter 7 bankruptcy. The merry-go-round of ownership and name changes continued over the next seventeen years (Banyan's, Eduardo's, Arizona 2400 and Il Tartufo). Since 2003, Chima Brazilian Steakhouse has occupied the site.

7

German

HEILMAN'S

The restaurant was originally opened as the Palmer House by Danny Palmer; it was later owned by George Menedis and then Joe Shinstock. Hubert Heilman purchased the property in 1958. Located at 1701 East Sunrise Boulevard, the restaurant's name was changed to Heilman's in 1960.

A third-generation restaurateur, Hubert Heilman got his start at his father's restaurant (founded 1920) in Lorain, Ohio. After graduating from the Cornell University School of Hotel Administration, he was operating both Heilman's locations in Lorian by 1958. In 1948, Heilman's brother Robert opened Heilman's Beachcomber in Clearwater, Florida, and in 1958, Hubert moved to Fort Lauderdale to open the family's fourth restaurant. According to a 1959 advertisement, the "chefs [were] dedicated to the use of pure ingredients…to cooking that gets its zip from nature's juices, real spices and herbs…to cooking that employs the finest meats, poultry and seafood obtainable." The 285-seat restaurant was a popular gathering place that offered cuisine from the family's Pennsylvania Dutch heritage, and Hubert's wife, Dorothy, managed the kitchen. Heilman's specialty was its "Back to the Farm" fried chicken. Plump pieces of chicken were rolled in flour and fried to a crisp golden brown in an old-fashioned cast-iron skillet loaded with butter (just like Grandma Heilman used to make). Heilman's was also known for its pine log baked potato and double-shot rum pie.

Exterior of Heilman's, with a sign that says, "Enjoy Our Famous Back to the Farm Fried Chicken Dinner." *Author's collection.*

During the off-season, the Heilmans would travel around the United States and the world to get new ideas for the restaurant. This led to a menu that was varied; it was cosmopolitan, continental, maritime and mid-American all at the same time. In 1962, the restaurant introduced the "yard of beer" glass. Heilman's was awarded the Golden Cup from the Coffee Brewing Center of the Pan-American Coffee Bureau for serving a "consistently outstanding cup of coffee over a period of five years" in 1968.

Hubert Heilman loved interacting with his patrons and bringing smiles to their faces. He instilled humor into the operation of the restaurant. A sign out front boasted that the place was "recommended by Hubert Heilman" and that the beverage list offered "the world's second-best martini." Heilman even got his friend Milton Berle, a comedian, to wait tables one day and nearly made a woman faint when Berle opened the front door and greeted her by name.

In 1975, Heilman sold the restaurant to George and Nick Telemachos, the owners of the Melbourne Beach Steak House. A stipulation of the sale was that the name had to be changed. Heilman did not want to be blamed or take credit for the new operation. Initially, the Telemachos just dropped the *i* (Helman's), but the restaurant was eventually renamed Helman's Brauhaus in 1981. Its new, revised menu featured *Deutsche spezialitaeten* (German specialties). In December 1986, the restaurant was again renamed to Sunrise Bar and Grill Restaurant. Today, a TD Bank is located on the site.

The Heilmans retired to Boca Raton, where Dorothy began painting and Hubert studied and wrote poetry. Their son, Ross (whose stage name was Ross Kananga), owned a large crocodile farm in Jamaica, where scenes for *Papillon* and *Live and Let Die* were shot. Ross was even Roger Moore's stunt double for the escape scene in which Moore's character runs across the crocodiles' backs in *Live and Let Die*.

STUDENT PRINCE

The Student Prince was opened in 1960 by Samuel and Monnie Chopman, who had previously owned and operated Lowery's Diner in Hollywood, Florida. In the two years before the Student Prince was opened, the building housed the Hudson Center Cafeteria (the first cafeteria in the Central Beach area); before that, it had housed the Sun and Sand Restaurant (1946–58), which was owned and operated by Joseph Hudson and Douglas Lockhart.

Interior view of the Student Prince, showing its alpine essence. *Author's collection.*

Paneled with teakwood, the Student Prince accentuated its Bavarian flavor with murals depicting scenes from the *Student Prince* operetta and the German and Italian Alps. The décor also featured beer steins and large cowbells that had been brought over from Europe. It was located along the Beach Strip at 229 South Atlantic Boulevard, just north of the Elbo Room.

Herman Odenweller owned the Student Prince from 1965 to 1969 before he sold it to his bartender, Erhard Schulz. The restaurant's German cuisine included bratwurst, knockwurst and bauernwurst, and it was popular among college kids, locals (especially German Americans) and European tourists alike. The Student Prince became a meeting place for the area's German visitors. "Some German customers…would tell their friends who were planning to visit Fort Lauderdale to come here if they didn't speak any English," said Schulz. "We could recommend hotels and help them make reservations."

In 1980, due to rising operating costs, Schulz sold the restaurant, and it became Andy Branagen's Eatery and Irish Pub. Today, Blondie's Sports Bar occupies the site.

8
Indian

MAHARAJA

Opened on November 17, 1973, the Maharaja replaced an Italian eatery at 127 Northwest Fortieth Avenue in the Westgate Shopping Center (Broward Boulevard and US 441). Owned by Dr. Jaswant Singh Pannu, an ophthalmologist, the restaurant grew out of the dinner parties that he hosted. "I had never been in the restaurant business before," Dr. Pannu said. "But when people came to our house, they always loved the food. Finally, our East Indian dinner parties grew bigger than we could handle."

The Maharaja was the first Indian restaurant in the state of Florida. Served by sari-clad waitresses with the sound of sitars in the background, Maharaja's selections included mulligatawny soup, tandoori chicken,

Opening week advertisement for the Maharaja, 1973. *Courtesy of the* Fort Lauderdale News.

shrimp bhoona, beef masala, mutter panner, jhinga bhuna, dhal, pellao and paratha. A belly dancer entertained guests on Thursday, Friday and Saturday nights.

By February 1976, the Maharaja was under new management, and it was closed by the end of that year. The Herb Cellar opened at the location in June 1977. Dr. Pannu continued his practice, inventing several instruments and intraocular lens implants that are still used in eye surgery. In 1993, he opened the Pannu Eye Institute.

9

Irish

SLY FOX

Built and opened by Benita Sirgany in late March 1974, the Sly Fox was a small and cozy English pub in a Tudor-style building. The pub's menu included an assortment of sandwiches, chicken dishes, shrimp and grouper tempura, open steak sandwiches, New York strips, steak tid-bits and eight-ounce hamburgers. Located at 3537 Galt Ocean Drive, the Sly Fox was, according to a 1985 *Fort Lauderdale News and Sun-Sentinel* article, "the place to go for people from their late twenties to early fifties" when it first opened. But by 1985, it was serving the condo crowd (late fifties to seventies). For the first twenty years of its existence, the Sly Fox changed operational management often; although, the name remained the same.

Stability in management came in 1993, when Danny Chichester purchased the Sly Fox and reopened it on January 1, 1994. Chichester worked as an accountant for legendary saloonkeeper Bernard "Toots" Shor in Manhattan, New York, during the mid-1960s. "That's where I got my real education," reminisced Chichester. "I learned to get my work done by 11:30 a.m., because that's when Toots would tell his office workers to get downstairs and start mingling with all the celebrities that were coming in. Of course, I learned to drink a bit from him too."

After a few years of operating his own bars in New York, Chichester relocated to Fort Lauderdale in 1968. "I had such a great time here during spring break in the early 1960s that I wanted to give running a business

Advertisement promoting that the Sly Fox is open for lunch, 1976. *Courtesy of the* Fort Lauderdale News.

a shot," he recalled. Between 1968 and 1974, Chichester opened eight Meyer's Pizzas across Broward County. He eventually sold those restaurants and started a chain of Danny's restaurants (two Fort Lauderdale locations, with others in Pompano, Coral Springs and Gainesville) as well as Runyon's and Chowder's in Coral Springs. By 1992, Chichester had sold or closed all of his locations; he wanted to only have one near his home on Galt Ocean Mile that he could operate and welcome old and new friends. The Sly Fox gave him that opportunity.

Under Chichester's management, the restaurant became an immediate success. The holiday buffets prepared by Chef Robert Wolff were legendary in the Fort Lauderdale hospitality industry. Galt Ocean Mile residents called the Sly Fox their second home, and it was not surprising to see Joe DiMaggio, Whitey Ford, past Dolphins players and other athletes, celebrities and local politicians sitting at the bar, talking old times with "Chi."

Chichester's dry wit and self-depreciating sense of humor endured him to all. Once, when he was asked, "Why are you drinking at this hour [9:00 a.m.]?" he replied, "Because I got started late." For all his joking, Chichester was usually right when it came to making decisions at the Sly Fox. "I figured out a pretty simple formula for success," he said. "Get yourself a good, friendly staff, a strong kitchen staff that is versatile and a pleasant neighborhood atmosphere, and you can be successful just about anywhere." Over the years, Chichester organized countless charity events and sponsored hundreds of youth league teams. During his last year at the Sly Fox (2002), Chichester ran a National Football League pool in which the winner was the one who had chosen the first team to have a player arrested.

In 2002, Martin Barrett purchased the Sly Fox, remodeled it and renamed it McGuinness' Bar and Restaurant. By 2009, he had changed the name to Barrett's Sly Fox Olde Irish Pub. It specialized in authentic Irish fare. "Fish and chips, bangers and mash and homemade soups were crowd favorites," stated general manager Robert Wolff in 2013. Barrett's Sly Fox was an official party spot for St. Patrick's Day. The holiday was preceded by a three-day Finnegan's Wake and a one-day "practice day" of drinking beforehand. Today, the building still stands, and in November 2019, it was reopened as Whale's Bar and Grill.

MAGUIRE'S HILL 16

Opened in the late 1980s at 535 North Andrews Avenue, Maguire's Hill 16 Pub and Eatery closed its doors on January 8, 2017. In its last eighteen years, Maguire's was owned by Jim and Martine Gregory and their son, James. It was Fort Lauderdale's oldest Irish pub and featured traditional Irish fare and live music.

The building was originally constructed in 1940 to house Browning's Grocery and Market. Over the years, it has been home to Andy's Grocery, Richard Mady's Bar, Mandray's Market, Frank's Café, Shorty's Bar, Shorty's Normandy Lounge, Fast Eddie's and Friday's Downtown. Maguire's was originally opened by Dubliner Alan Craig and his wife, Hilary. Craig also owned the Irish Times Pub (Palm Beach Gardens), Finnegan's Wake (Key West) and Fiddler's Green (Winter Park), and he was the front man for Maguire's house band, the Irish Times. The Gregorys purchased the pub in 1999.

South exterior and main entrance of Maguire's Hill 16. *Courtesy of the* Sun-Sentinel.

Maguire's was an old-school Irish pub, and the Gregorys felt that it was very important "that everyone who [walked] through [their] doors [experienced] the hospitality and a bit of the culture they would find back home in Ireland." The pub was popular with locals and tourists, both Irish and honorary Irish. Maguire's was a favorite lunch spot for downtown professionals, including many from the legal and law enforcement professions. The pub was where patrons gathered for birthdays, retirements and wakes. Maguire's was also a place to watch football and soccer games. Fans of the Pittsburgh Steelers, Baltimore Ravens and Notre Dame Fighting Irish all claimed the pub as their team's Fort Lauderdale headquarters.

Serving a mix of Irish and American cuisine, Maguire's was known for its potato soup, fish and chips, bangers 'n' mash, lamb stew and shepherd's pie. Jennifer L. commented on Yelp, "Absolutely the most delicious corned beef and cabbage I have ever had! My husband's shepherd's pie was also delicious! The portions were huge, and prices are great for the area!" St. Patrick's Day was always a big event at Maguire's. It started with breakfast at 7:00 a.m., and its music and festivities lasted until midnight. With four thousand to five thousand patrons during the day, it was regarded as the biggest and best St. Patrick's Day party in South Florida.

In late 2018, the Gregorys sold Maguire's to the Restaurant People, a hospitality group that operates many establishments around Fort Lauderdale. At the time of this writing, no plans have been announced for the site. Most of the patrons were saddened by the news of Maguire's closing. As Pia Dahlquist commented, "I'm going to feel homeless. I've been coming here at least once or twice a week for the last three decades. This is a place where you could come by yourself and be comfortable. You just feel at home." After closing the pub, the Gregorys returned to County Kildare, Ireland, where they operate several pubs today.

10

Italian

TINA'S SPAGHETTI HOUSE

Tina's Spaghetti House, which was located at 2110 South Federal Highway, was originally opened in 1946 as Jack and Ernie's Spaghetti House. Gus Ducas (Kostantinos Doucakos), the restaurant's original owner, moved to Fort Lauderdale in 1946 and operated the restaurant until 1956. He also helped to start St. Demetrois Greek Orthodox Church. In 1951, Ducas changed the name to Tina's after his wife, Tina (Athena). The restaurant was sold to Kenneth Biebel in 1956. Ironically, the Italian restaurant was transferred from a Greek owner to a German owner. Ducas later owned and operated Topper's restaurant (1958–61).

Tina's Spaghetti House was known for stuffing families with mounds of Italian food at some of the most reasonable prices in town. Marcia Marcho-Denius remarked, "This was my favorite place. Their creamy garlic salad dressing and garlic bread were to die for. I always ordered spaghetti with meat sauce and mushrooms." Sherry Davis Lucas concurred, "Antipasto and veal parmesan—never had any better." In the mid-1950s, the restaurant even hosted art exhibitions. By 1960, newspaper advertisements were touting Tina's as "Fort Lauderdale's Oldest Spaghetti House." This little neighborhood Italian restaurant always relied on the local crowd, not the fickle tourists, and it made its customers feel like family. Nevra Coffin-Schiavon remembers, "[I] loved date nights that began at Tina's! Great food and a welcoming staff." The

The staff of Tina's Spaghetti House. *Author's collection.*

waitresses were friendly and knew most of the regulars; they never forgot a face. Many were devoted members of the family. Irene Doerfler was there at the beginning (1946) and dished out spaghetti for thirty-four years. At the time of her retirement, two other waitresses had been at Tina's for over a decade and another had been there for twenty years. In 1985, Kitty Mossey retired after twenty-five years.

Even though Tina's was a neighborhood eatery, on occasion, celebrities would stop by. Kitty Mossey recalls actors Susan Hayward and Johnny Weissmuller visiting several times. On March 5, 1980, Prince Andrew, Duke of York and midshipman of the HMS *Hermes* (docked at Port Everglades), and several of his shipmates were spotted dining at Tina's.

The Biebels (Ken and later his son Barry) owned the restaurant until the mid-1980s. Afterward, it passed through several owners until Frank "Butch" Samp, the owner of the Floridian Restaurant and, later, Ernie's Bar-B-Q, bought Tina's in 1996. Tina's Spaghetti House was closed a few years later.

GINA'S ITALIAN

Opening around 1946 at 4331 South Ravenswood Road, along the Dania Cut-Off Canal, Gina's offered home-cooked Italian food. Owner Gina Riva kept a menagerie of animals on the property; in addition to chickens, ducks, peacocks, a donkey and a horse, she maintained a small alligator pit to entertain her customers. Gina even had a goat named Guiseppi Garabaldi II who "played" the piano. Gina's animals lured visitors from far and wide.

The restaurant's featured attraction was Suzette, a 350-pound Poland China pig with an appetite for spaghetti and a thirst for scotch and soda. Suzette was also known to drink beer. One of her admirers was Arthur Godfrey, a nationally known radio personality who was reported to have said that Gina's served the "best Italian food in Florida." He continued, saying, "There is nothing like a nice comfortable dinner with a pig in the parlor." Gina allowed her animals to roam freely, much to the consternation of her neighbors. Eventually, she had to pen them all up. Suzette, once a staple inside the restaurant, ultimately had to be kept outdoors due to sanitation codes.

On December 8, 1956, a grand opening was held for Gina's Rustic Inn under the new management of Henry Oreal, William Cailini and Wayne McDonald. The restaurant's name was changed to the Rustic Inn Crab House once crabs became the featured menu item. It is still open to this day.

Owner Gina Riva feeding her pigs outside of the restaurant. *Author's collection.*

JOHNNY'S EL DORADO

Johnny's El Dorado, an Italian restaurant, was owned and operated for thirty years by John Samuel Ferracane. The son of Italian immigrants from Palermo, Sicily, John was born in Brooklyn, where his parents, Benedetto and Maria, owned Ferracane's Italian Bakery.

In 1948, following his service in World War II and eventual discharge from the army signal corps, John, with his parents, brother (Frank) and sister (Jeanie) moved to Fort Lauderdale. There, the family opened Maria's Pizzeria. The following year, on April 9, John and his wife, Anne, opened El Dorado's Restaurant at 721 North Federal Highway. It featured an Italian American menu, and Mr. Ferracane cooked much of the food himself. The restaurant's specialties were spaghetti with lobster sauce, ziti Sicilian and super-manicotti that was handmade by Momma Maria.

The El Dorado remained at the same location for about eight years before moving to 2535 North Federal Highway in 1956. On October 13 of that year, the new Johnny's El Dorado was opened. Mr. Ferracane operated the restaurant until 1978, when he sold it and moved to Altamonte Springs,

Opening announcement for the new location of Johnny's Eldorado, 1956. *Courtesy of the* Fort Lauderdale Daily News.

Florida, to pursue other business interests. The restaurant later became Pasquale's Italian Restaurant, and, today, the site is occupied by a Ruth's Chris Steak House.

LA PERLA

Vincenzo Di Leo moved to Fort Lauderdale from Fallo, Italy, in the late 1970s, so that his wife could be closer to her family in Miami. Di Leo had worked as a waiter in Italy; his first restaurant was nothing more than a glorified hot dog stand at 1818 East Sunrise Boulevard. He and his brother and partner, Anthony, gradually transformed the stand into a fine-dining establishment worthy of praise as an exceptional Italian restaurant by food critics. Treats included pappardelle bolognese and ziti all'ortolana. La Perla was conveniently located for Gateway Theater and Shopping Center patrons, and it was extremely comfortable with its non-pretentious atmosphere. "My father was a very service-oriented person. The way he welcomed people, it was like they were in his living room," recalled his son, Massimiliano.

Around 1985, Vincenzo decided to return to Italy, so he sold his share of the restaurant to his brother, Anthony, and Dominick La Croix. In 1989, he returned to Fort Lauderdale, where Tony and Dom had opened an additional restaurant, Il Mulino, on the same block. Vincenzo became a

Ristorante Italiano
La Perla
CUISINE
EXTRAORDINARY
DINNER ONLY
RESERVATIONS
765-1950
Your Host Vincenzo
1818 E. Sunrise Blvd., Fort Lauderdale
Open Daily

La Perla advertisement, 1980. *Courtesy of the* Fort Lauderdale News.

59

partner in both restaurants and managed La Perla until his death in May 1994. Following Vincenzo's passing, Anthony brought on his son, Mario, as a co-owner. By January 1995, Mario and his partner, Chris Wilber, had renovated La Perla and renamed it Canyon Southwest Café, an upscale southwestern-style eatery featuring Tex-Mex cuisine.

BRAVO RISTORANTE

Bravo Ristorante was opened in June 1991 at 1515 Southeast Seventeenth Street Causeway in the Quay Shopping Center; it closed unexpectedly on June 13, 2019. Providing a warm ambiance, with friendly service, brick walls and rustic lighting, this 175-seat restaurant was an authentic Italian trattoria–style eatery. Russ Dickson, the general manager and, later, partner (1998) and sole owner (2010), said the secret to Bravo's longevity was its consistency, quality and top-notch service. The restaurant's chef had been

Executive Chef, Jimmy Henriquez, and proprietor, Russ Dickson, of Bravo Ristorante, 2012. *Photographed by Candace West. Courtesy of* Broward/Palm Beach New Times.

there since the beginning, and most of the kitchen's employees had been there between eight and ten years.

The restaurant featured an extensive menu of pasta dishes (over two dozen), nearly twenty veal and chicken entrées, thin-crust pizzas and ocean-fresh seafood. These selections were accompanied by a full bar and well-rounded wine list. The restaurant's garlic rolls were super delicious. Ariana Waschler remarked, "Superior Italian food in the Fort Lauderdale area. Every pasta dish I have had was cooked to perfection with homemade authentic Italian taste! The garlic rolls are a must—so delicious! Number one choice for Italian food in Broward County." Jan McAndrew Henry concurred, "The very best fried calamari salad ever, and their chicken parm with angel hair pasta [is] just so awesome! I cannot believe they are closed! Loved their food. They would also do a special pizza for me with mussels! Sad!" In addition to traditional dinner service, Bravo Ristorante offered happy hour from 4:00 to 7:00 p.m. every weekday. This special included discount prices on appetizers (seven dollars), entrées (fourteen dollars) and wine and well drinks (six dollars). Bill Bierbower stated, "I will miss their happy hour meals."

With the restaurant's lease expiring, high projected costs for upgrades under a new lease and rising daily business costs, Dickson decided to pull the plug. Increased competition from other eating places along the Seventeenth Street Causeway and other Italian restaurants on Las Olas Boulevard (three new ones had opened in 2019, resulting in twelve total on the street) was also a contributing factor to the restaurant's closure.

11

Jewish

WOLFIE'S

Wolfie's Restaurant was part of a regional New York City–style delicatessen chain that was started by Wilfred "Wolfie" Cohen in Miami Beach in 1947. After making the deli successful, he sold it and the name to Meyer Yedlin in 1948. Yedlin opened two additional locations in Miami and another in St. Petersburg. Yedlin and his partner, Joseph Sloane, opened Wolfie's Fort Lauderdale location in February 1959. Located at 2501 East Sunrise Boulevard in the Sunrise Plaza, across from the Sunrise Shopping Center (today the Galleria Mall), Wolfie's sat about 235 customers and employed 100. All of the deli's food was prepared on the premises, including its bread and the beef for its hamburgers. Wolfie's featured a main dining room, a private dining room, fountain service, a kitchen, a bakery and pantry and a unique room called the Wolf's Den. The main dining room had counter service as well as booth and table service. The Wolf's Den looked like a cavern with a service bar and wall benches.

Wolfie's was Fort Lauderdale's most popular deli and featured an extensive menu. According to the menu, it was "an old established tradition for fine Kosher-style cooking...the best of Jewish-American cuisine." A bowl of coleslaw and dill pickles were set out on every table. Wolfie's catered to everyone, whether they were local residents, snowbirds or tourists. Kimberly Weed Hope remembered, "Great childhood memories of Sunday breakfasts there!" Elaine Conn posted on Facebook, "The best pickles and coleslaw, corned beef sandwiches AND desserts!"

Two-part postcard showing the interior and exterior of Wolfie's on Sunrise Boulevard. *Author's collection.*

When it opened in 1959, Wolfie's was open from 7:00 a.m. to 2:00 a.m. daily (3:00 a.m. on Saturday). Eventually, the deli was open until 3:00 a.m. on Fridays as well. In addition to sit-down and take-out service, Wolfie's also provided catering. In January 1971, Wolfie's received a special award from the Fort Lauderdale Jaycees for sponsoring eight years of free dinners for underprivileged children during the Jaycees' annual Christmas shopping tour for the children.

On April 10, 1986, owners Robert and William Galante unexpectedly closed the restaurant. Competition from the Carnegie Deli in the Galleria and a two-year closing of part of the Sunrise Boulevard Bridge clearly affected business. Meyer's Deli of Canada opened at the site in March 1987, but it didn't last the year. Beginning in 1996, the building housed Wild Oats Community Market (later Natural Martketplace) for about a decade. Since July 2011, the location has housed a Publix supermarket.

12

Southern

CLARK'S DINING ROOM

Annie Clark arrived in Fort Lauderdale with her family in 1904. Since she was an excellent cook, Annie opened a small dining room at the foot of Brickell Avenue, on the edge of the New River, and operated it during the first decade of the twentieth century. After her husband was bitten and killed by a rattlesnake in 1917, she bought a house at the southwest corner of Southeast Second Street and Second Avenue.

As a widow with four sons, including longtime Broward County sheriff Walter Clark and chief deputy Robert Clark, Ann began taking in boarders and converted the first floor of her home into a diner. There, she served

Exterior of Clark's Dining Room at Southeast Second Avenue and Second Street. *Courtesy of the Broward County Historical Archives, Broward County Library, Clark Family Collection.*

hearty, home-cooked meals. The price of a full breakfast was seventeen cents, and dinners were all-you-can-eat for fifty cents. Customers were not only attracted by the diner's prices, but they were also attracted by the aromas that wafted out of the open kitchen windows.

Mrs. Clark operated the dining room until 1935, when she sold it to I. Gordon Cranton, the former owner of the Dixie Cafeteria on Brickell Avenue and Cranton's Barbecue at Las Olas Beach (site of the Elbo Room today). Cranton ran the diner until 1944. Mrs. Clark passed in September 1937. Today, the Riverwalk Center Parking Garage is located at the site.

PIONEER HOUSE

Following the death of her husband, Frank Stranahan (the Father of Fort Lauderdale), in 1929, and in the midst of the Great Depression, Ivy Stranahan rented out her home (now the Historic Stranahan House Museum, which was built in 1901 by Ed King) to boarders. In 1933, Mrs. Clifton Breckenridge turned the first floor of the home into a restaurant, the Casa Basque, and operated it for two seasons. During the 1935–6 and 1936–7 seasons, Mrs. Miller Ward managed the restaurant as the Water's Edge Inn. On January 1, 1939, Mr. and Mrs. Ernest Vivian reopened the restaurant as the Swiss Chalet.

Etson and Elsie Blackwell were married in 1924 and operated the Rockery Tea Room on Young Circle in Hollywood, Florida. During a drive up Federal Highway, in 1939, they noticed a "for rent" sign on the Stranahan

View of the exterior of the Pioneer House, looking north from the New River. *Courtesy of the State Archives of Florida, Florida Memory.*

House (located on the northwest bank of the New River at the Federal Highway Bridge) and approached Ivy about opening up another restaurant. Ivy agreed, and the Blackwells occupied the first floor of the home. They expanded and enclosed the south porch, which extended the dining area all the way to the river.

The Pioneer House Restaurant opened in 1940, with an eccentric sign along the New River that read "Since 1893" (when Frank Stranahan arrived at the site). It served southern-style food and was a popular Sunday dinner destination for families. "It was a very popular place, a well-loved place," said Joyce Blackwell Martin, Mr. Blackwell's daughter. "You could sit by the water and see the boats go under the bridge."

The restaurant remained open until 1979, when the Fort Lauderdale Historical Society purchased the building. They renovated the 1901 structure (which was placed on the National Register of Historic Places in 1973), and in 1984, it was opened as a 1915-era historic house museum. It still functions as such today.

CREIGHTON'S

In the early 1950s, Charles Creighton arrived in Fort Lauderdale from North Carolina, where he had opened his first restaurant around 1940. Creighton quickly became an important community figure in Fort Lauderdale. In 1955, he opened Creighton's Restaurant next to the Sunrise Shopping Center (which was opened in January 1954). Later that year, he purchased the outdoor mall from Antioch College.

Located on the west bank of the Intracoastal Waterway, at Sunrise Boulevard, the twelve-thousand-square-foot restaurant eventually featured five separate dining rooms: the Sevres, the Venetian, the Gazebo, the Cybis Room and the Jade Room. The locale boasted "ample parking for both yachts and automobiles." One of the highlights of visiting Creighton's, aside from its waterfront views, was its collection of art and antiques that it displayed. It is estimated that the collection was valued at over $2.5 million and included French crystal chandeliers, Chinese jade, Russian paintings and tables and paintings from Napoleon's palace (Palace of Fontainebleau).

Proclaiming itself as "one of the finest restaurants in America" (postcard reverse), with excellent service, Creighton's served down-home, southern-style cuisine. Creighton's also touted an "unusually large variety of foods to

Home of the "World's Best Apple Pie," Creighton's also housed over $2.5 million worth of art and antiques. *Courtesy of the Broward County Historical Archives, Broward County Library.*

choose from." The restaurant prepared and cooked all of its food in its own kitchen, and it made its hot rolls and pastries in its own bakeshop. You could choose everything, from a petite filet mignon to a twenty-ounce porterhouse and a selection of tantalizing roasts, fowl and seafood. Creighton's became famous for its "world's best apple pie" (as touted by a huge neon sign on the building); the pie even received a compliment from Duncan Hines. "Recommended by everyone as America's showplace," Creighton's was an attraction for locals and tourists. It was a place for locals to celebrate special occasions, and it was where out-of-town visitors—even King Saud of Saudi Arabia—would dine.

In the late 1970s, Charles Creighton sold the restaurant and the Sunrise Shopping Center for approximately $13 million. It was redeveloped as the Galleria Mall; today, the GALLERYone, a DoubleTree Suites hotel, sits on the restaurant's former site.

PART 2

SURF AND TURF

Going to a restaurant is one of my keenest pleasures. Meeting someplace with old and new friends, ordering wine, eating food, surrounded by strangers—I think is the core of what it means to live a civilized life.
—Adam Gopnik

Since Fort Lauderdale is located at the confluence of the Atlantic Ocean and the New River, it has historically had an ample supply of saltwater and freshwater fish and shellfish. As an early agricultural locale, the restaurants in the town also had access to locally grown fresh fruits and vegetables. Although much of the area's aquatic meat and produce was shipped north, via the Florida East Coast Railroad and ships out of Port Everglades, plenty of the supply remained in town for the local eateries. The railroad and, later, the port brought beef and pork in during the first half of the twentieth century. Poultry (chicken and turkey) was grown locally. Following World War II, foodstuffs arrived in Fort Lauderdale via train, truck, plane and boat.

Steakhouses and seafood restaurants have been staples of the Fort Lauderdale dining scene since the early days of the city. Some of these restaurants have been mundane, some have been exquisite and there have been many in between, but they have all served quality meals, with various individual selections and combinations. Locals, Americans from other states and international visitors who arrived on airplanes and cruise ships have sampled many of these culinary delights.

Welcome Back . . .
THE FABULOUS
YANKEES
"Thanks Again"
JIMMY FAZIO'S
HOUSE OF PRIME RIBS
FT. LAUDERDALE'S BRIGHTEST SPOT
3485 N. Federal Hwy. — Ft. Lauderdale
● **FOR THE BEST IN FOOD**
The World's Finest
Prime Ribs & Steak Dinners
SERVING 12 NOON TO 4 A.M.
★ **Florida's Biggest Entertainment Policy** ★

Don't Forget — Open for Luncheons Daily Except Sat.

Reservations: Phone 565-4102 or 565-4146

Jimmy Fazio's House of Prime Ribs advertisement welcoming back the New York Yankees for spring training in 1966. *Courtesy of the* Fort Lauderdale News.

The Burgundy Restaurant advertised that it "specialized in Southern fried chicken, steaks, chops and sea foods," and the Fisherman Restaurant and Bar touted itself as serving "South Florida's finest gourmet seafood." The Fisherman specialized in fresh fish, lobster, raw oysters and clams. The New River Tea Room was "famous for steaks" and "delicious meals served in delightful surroundings." Other popular steak and seafood eateries in Fort Lauderdale were the Terrace Patio, the Town House, the Crab Pot, Dante's, Harrison's on the Water, the Fin 'N' Haddie and Gibby's Steak and Seafood.

13
Seafood

THE BEACHCOMBER

Russ and Clara Wilson moved to Fort Lauderdale from Carteret, New Jersey, in 1941. Russ had served as a chief steward with the U.S. Merchant Marines for twenty-five years, and Clara had worked at the famous Schrafft's Restaurant in New York City. In 1942, the couple opened the Beachcomber Restaurant at 2915 East Las Olas Boulevard. In the 1930s, the building was home to Jimmie Vreeland's Freshest Fish Market, and in the early 1940s, it was home to Vreeland's Good Sea Foods.

Russ was the cook at the Beachcomber. The restaurant's biggest sellers were red snapper, chicken and dumplings and roast beef. In its early days, Captain James B. Vreeland Jr., Fort Lauderdale's most knowledgeable fisherman, was the Beachcomber's exclusive provider of fish. The Beachcomber touted that its seafood was cooked and served only a few hours after it was taken from the sea. The restaurant received its liquor license in August 1944, "over the objections of C.A. Luce, owner and operator of the Intracoastal Apartments on Birch Road."

Located just past the Las Olas Bridge, the Beachcomber was known as the place where gourmets met by a generation of famous travelers. The restaurant's "regular" celebrity patrons included Lauritz Melchoir (pre-eminent Wagnerian tenor of the 1920s and 1940s), Irene Dunne (actress with five Oscar nominations), Ben Duffy (president of the Batten, Barton, Durstine and Osborn advertising agency) and Jean Paul St. Laurent (son of Canada's prime minister Louis St. Laurent).

In 1948, the restaurant began operating with an open summer schedule in cooperation with the Beach Improvement Association and the City of Fort Lauderdale, which were attempting to make the town a year-round resort. In a May 25, 1948 *Fort Lauderdale Daily News* advertisement, the Beachcomber thanked its patrons:

> *Your reception and acceptance of our new summer policy for fine food and drink, at truly moderate prices, has been absolutely amazing.*
>
> *Think of it! Those famed Beachcomber quality dinners for as low as $1.25—refreshing and cooling cocktails at 50 cents—and those delightful, fragrant ocean breezes to add to your dining comfort. You just can't beat a summer bargain, such as this!*
>
> *So, come on out tonight and every night—and get acquainted with, by far, the best eat and drink value in all of South Florida.*

In 1950, the Wilsons opened a complementary restaurant, the 'Comber, at 2941 East Las Olas Boulevard; it served sandwiches, breakfast, lunch and

Interior view of the original Beachcomber restaurant on Las Olas Boulevard. *Courtesy of the Broward County Historical Archives, Broward County Library, Vreeland Collection.*

dinner. Through the 1950s, the Beachcomber hosted and provided a buffet dinner for an annual auction for the March of Dimes. At the restaurant, Clara always greeted children personally and gave each and every one a little toy or present.

In 1956, the City of Fort Lauderdale wanted to widen Las Olas Boulevard. Wilson successfully sued the city and received $23,862 in damages for the loss of facilities and business due to the street work. The Wilsons then relocated the Beachcomber to the new Coral Shopping Center on the southwest corner of U.S. 1 and Oakland Park Boulevard.

In early 1961, Clara passed away, and Russ sold the Beachcomber. He later opened the Club House at the Farmer's Market in Pompano Beach in October 1961. He passed away in early January 1962. The Beachcomber was purchased by Dr. Emilio Nunez Portuondo, a former ambassador and permanent representative of Cuba to the United Nations, and Rafael Garcia Navarro, a former chief of Cuba's economic mission to the United Nations. Both men had been ousted from Cuba when Fidel Castro took power. They renamed the restaurant the El Madrid. The original Beachcomber site is now home to the Nanou French Bakery and Café.

GRIFFITH'S OYSTER BAR

Originally located at 3001 South Federal Highway, Griffith's Oyster Bar was opened in 1946. Established by Russell and Edith Griffith, it was the first oyster bar in Broward County. Russell arrived in Fort Lauderdale from Indianapolis, Indiana, in 1935, and Edith's family (Gauld) arrived in the area in 1936. The Gauld's owned the Lauderdale Trailer Camp at 3301 South Andrews Avenue. In 1948, the Griffiths moved their restaurant to 3301 South Andrews Avenue. Griffith's Oyster Bar was housed in a wood-frame and clapboard structure that had been moved to the site from Port Everglades. It had formerly been a naval office building during World War II. The Griffiths old location became the Carolina County Oyster Bar, but it did not remain open for very long.

In the early years, Griffith's advertised itself as "Broward County's only oyster bar," and it offered a daily seafood special, baked stuffed shrimp, a seafood platter and, of course, oysters on the half shell. Chincoteague oysters were the restaurant's specialty. Later additions to the menu included lobster (from both Florida and Maine), filet mignon, chicken and frog legs.

OPENING FOR THE SEASON

TODAY

GRIFFITH'S

Seafoods OUR SPECIALTY

★ Oysters & Clams ON THE HALF SHELL
★ Fried Chicken
★ Western Steaks

Oyster Bar

BROWARD COUNTY'S ORIGINAL

Florida Lobster
All You Can Eat $2.00

3301 S. ANDREWS AVE.,
FORT LAUDERDALE

Advertisement for the opening of the 1952–53 tourist season. *Courtesy of the Fort Lauderdale Daily News.*

Bill the Bartender's signature drink, the "Salty Dog" (whiskey with unsweetened grapefruit juice, salted to taste), was very popular.

Russell would lay his own lobster traps off the Dania beach and use portions of the catch in the restaurant. In 1958, Russell became the first president of the Broward County Commercial Lobster Co-operative, which was tasked with developing antipoaching and trap stealing strategies. He passed away in October 1961. Edith kept running the restaurant until she sold it in 1977. In the late 1960s, she served as the second vice-president of the Broward County Restaurant Association. Edith passed away in 2002.

In December 1977, Griffith's Oyster Bar was scheduled to reopen under new owner Ciro Nessuno when it suffered a fire. Nessuno decided not to continue with the restaurant and opened Ciro's Quality Office Furniture at the location (which went out of business in 1980). The Airport 595 Business Center can be found at the site today.

SEA GRILL LOUNGE AND RESTAURANT

First located at the corner of Sunrise Boulevard and Sixteenth Terrace, the Sea Grill Lounge and Restaurant was opened by Edward Wolchick Sr. in 1959. Wolchick had come to Broward County from Washington, D.C. The family-owned and -operated restaurant remained open for twenty-eight years, and it was closed down in 1987. The restaurant was patterned after the O'Donnell's Sea Grill in Washington, D.C. (its founder, Tom O'Donnell, was Edward's father-in-law).

In 1964, after the restaurant took off, the Wolchicks moved it to 1619 Northeast Fourth Avenue (the former home of Jack Campbell's Restaurant, Ming's Chinese Food and Harley's Steak House), across the street from the newly opened (1962) Fort Lauderdale High School. Scott Mercer posted

Three-part postcard showing the interior and exterior signage of the Sea Grill, 1960s. *Author's Collection.*

on Facebook, "I had an English teacher that would have a few cocktails in their bar for lunch. We had the class right after…whoopee." The Sea Grill advertised that all meals were served with its "original Rum Buns." A 1964 review of the restaurant in the *Fort Lauderdale News* raved about its Baltimore-style deviled crab, clam chowder, Key lime pie and uncommonly crisp and cold green salad. This landmark seafood restaurant was also known for its green turtle steak sautéed in butter with garlic.

The Sea Grill had a strong following that included families and local lunchtime politicians. "I would go at lunch time," former Wilton Manors mayor Tracy Stafford said. "And you'd always run into some political types in there—you know, the Oakland Park, Wilton Manors, Fort Lauderdale crowd." A 1980 restaurant guide in the *Fort Lauderdale News* described the restaurant as "a comfortable, high-volume fish house that's built its loyal clientele of twenty years by providing only the best and the freshest—lunch and dinner—moderate to expensive."

When the restaurant closed in 1987, an auction of everything in the building was held. Former customers and other restaurateurs could purchase logo items, paintings, ship models, barstools and kitchen equipment. Many locals lamented the closing. "We've been going to the Sea Grill since it was on Sunrise. We were regulars, and it was nice to come and be recognized. We never thought it would close," said Evelyn Kadala. Mark Martin mentioned on Facebook, "My parents brought us there every weekend for years in the 1970s. Man, I'd give anything to have an imperial crab platter with coleslaw again. I've never matched it anywhere." Today, the building houses the Fort Lauderdale Community School, which teaches GED and ESOL classes.

OLD FLORIDA SEAFOOD HOUSE

Although Old Florida Seafood House was not technically in Fort Lauderdale (it was located a few blocks across the city line, at 1414 Northeast Twenty-Sixth Street in Wilton Manors), there is no doubt that it was truly one of the top seafood and social establishments in the area for over thirty-five years.

Originally an A&P Supermarket and, later, a family steakhouse, the restaurant was opened in August 1977 by Bob Wickline and Mike Swanson, and it immediately became one of the premier seafood restaurants in all of Broward County and beyond. "We were known for our raw bar, oysters, clams and shrimp," claimed one waitress who worked there for twenty-eight years. "Fried shrimp and shrimp de jonghe (a baked casserole with garlic breadcrumbs) were very popular with my regulars, and many would order a selection of appetizers just to have a taste of everything on the menu." Chef Gustav would prepare imaginative seafood (snapper, shrimp, salmon and lobster) dishes with a touch of New Orleans. The fresh catch was always good and could be ordered broiled; sautéed; fried; Française-style, with marinara; or spicy Cajun-style. Two long-standing sides that were not to be missed were the twice-baked potato, with a touch of garlic and parsley, and the fried zucchini, with a tempura coating.

In its first ten years of operation, the Old Florida Seafood House was located next to the Manor Art Cinema, so patrons could stop for dinner and a show. One of the unique features of the Old Florida Seafood House was a private bar area that was simply called the Den, which was very popular with employees of other restaurants, hotels and other hospitality businesses. "You had to be a member to get a pass key to get into the back room, or you could go in once or twice with a member," recalled a former waitress. "It was really set up to take care of the ITB (In-The-Bar Biz) crowd. There was a special menu with discounted drinks and food, and the bartender, 'Butter,' knew everyone and what they drank. The members

Exterior of the defunct Old Florida Seafood House. *Author's collection.*

would bring guests or tell their customers about the food, and it was a great way to bring in new business."

Voted one of Florida's top one hundred restaurants by *Florida Trend* and recommended by the *Mobil Guide* and the *Florida Restaurant Guide*, the Old Florida Seafood House had a history of pleasing its customers. Nate from San Diego stated on Yelp, "Good ole fashioned seafood house in South Florida! This place is definitely a throwback to the 1970s. They try hard to make sure to satisfy any seafood craving you may be having! Salads are great, breads keep coming and service is friendly." Rori Parson concurred, "Best fried shrimp, fried zucchini and blueberry muffins! Used to drive over on the alley from Fort Myers Beach to have dinner." According to Susan McLean Colantuoni, "Our family favorite! Their Florida stuffed lobster tail was the best ever! Conch chowder was authentic Florida-style."

In its later years, the restaurant was getting old—both its décor and patrons. Wickline and Swanson eventually sold the restaurant to an inexperienced couple and a friend from Wilton Manors in September 2013. The restaurant did not last a year before closing down; this was largely due to its poor-quality food, bad service and management infighting. The restaurant updated its décor, but its prices went up and portion sizes went down. The building has been empty since then.

SHIRTTAIL CHARLIE'S

Not to be confused with an earlier Shirttail Charlie's that operated from 1963 to 1965 at 1791 West Broward Boulevard, the seafood restaurant Shirttail Charlie's was located on the New River, at 400 Southwest Third Avenue. Doug Mackle opened the restaurant in 1984. He was a graduate of the Florida International University School of Hotel, Food and Travel Services, and he was a former co-owner of the Takeyama and Mackle Japanese Restaurant. He also bought Le Dôme in 1988. Shirttail Charlie's was located at the Riverfront Marina, on the south bank of the New River, in approximately the same spot where Reed Bryan constructed the dredges *Everglades* and *Okeechobee* in 1906, which cut the canals to drain the Everglades. Ed King's boatyard was later situated in this same area.

Built to look like old-style Florida architecture, Shirttail Charlie's featured a raw bar, a dockside bar, a swimming pool, twenty-five boat slips and comfortable decks with benches. The restaurant was named after Shirttail Charlie Tommie, a Seminole native and fixture in downtown Fort Lauderdale during the 1910s and 1920s. Charlie would panhandle for "drink" money

Exterior of Shirttail Charlie's from the New River, 2005. *Courtesy of Ron Dougherty.*

and take pictures with tourists; he also wore a traditional Seminole long shirt, hence his nickname.

After opening on October 30, 1984, with over five hundred guests, Shirttail Charlie's specialized in fresh-caught Florida fish that was prepared to order from a selection of southern recipes. The menu also featured shrimp, conch, scallops, steak, hammock-style chicken, barbecued pork chops, shark bites, sautéed alligator, Seminole rice, Caloosa slaw and Key Lime pie. A favorite dessert of many of the restaurant's patrons was its homemade walnut brownie topped with vanilla ice cream and hot fudge. Bonnie Petty thought the restaurant had the "best conch fritters around!"

Advertised as "hard to find…but worth the effort," the restaurant provided waterfront views of New River boats, the Florida East Coast Railway trains and downtown Fort Lauderdale. In addition to providing individual boat dockage, the site also served as a water taxi stop. For many years, Shirttail Charlie's also offered free after-dinner river cruises for its patrons, and it hosted an annual dolphin fishing tournament for charity. Over the years the restaurant became a well-known destination for locals, boaters and tourists. As Derek Mejia remembered, Shirttail Charlie's was a "great place on the water to drink and chill out!" However, in 2007, the restaurant closed, as its property's landlord had plans to redevelop the site. Those plans eventually fell through, and in 2009, the restaurant reopened as the Pirate Republic Bar and Grill.

14
Steakhouses

TALE O' THE TIGER

In the mid-1950s, restaurants were rapidly moving into the strip of land along North Federal Highway, between the Gateway Shopping Center (Sunrise Boulevard) and Oakland Park Boulevard. One of these restaurants, which was situated next to the Sherwood Motel, was the Tale o' the Tiger. Located at 2205 North Federal, this restaurant and lounge had a menu that featured roast prime rib of beef and, according to a *Fort Lauderdale News* advertisement from 1956, is "a tale of unforgettable food exquisitely served in an atmosphere of charm and friendly warmth."

Owned and operated by Walter "Rocky" Roncaglione, a former Washington, D.C. restaurateur, the Tale o' the Tiger was opened on February 11, 1956. It contained a dining room (150-person capacity), a cocktail lounge (elevated with sectional furniture), a coffee shop, a huge kitchen and a parking area for more than one hundred cars. The walls were adorned with murals that depicted scenes from the history of the Flying Tigers (the American volunteer pilots who fought in China against the Japanese during World War II), including images of tigers, a Chinese junk, rice paddies, a C-47 and P-40s. Rocky had served with the Flying Tigers as support personnel and had been in charge of housing, food and entertainment for them throughout the war.

In 1957, Roncaglione partnered with Nicholas, John and Spiro Yianilos and Peter and George Vezos to form what became the Ranch House chain.

Tale o' the Tiger menu cover (1960s), with inset advertisement of Jay Wray "Mr. Funderful" and Miss Julie Barry, entertainers. *Courtesy of the* Fort Lauderdale News.

They also partnered in owning the Tale o' the Tiger and the Sherwood Motel. Tale o' the Tiger was briefly (from August 1957 to July 1958) owned by Clarence Sieger and his son-in-law, Bruna Bieluwka, before Roncaglione's group bought it back. J. Roy Fink was brought on as manager and co-owner in August 1958. Maine lobster, prime rib and charcoal broiled steaks were the restaurant's featured menu items.

Tale o' the Tiger was sold in 1973; it became Rip's in 1974 and Tiger's Tale in 1975 before finally closing. The Caves, which was owned by Saul Hochman, later opened at that location. Today, the Vitamin Shoppe is located there.

RAIN DANCER SIRLOIN PIT AND TAVERN

In January 1972, the Rain Dancer was opened at the former site of Charles W. Morgan Seafood; it was owned by Frank Callander, Bruce Grassfield and Bill Brattain. The men had six similar operations in Montreal, New York, Rhode Island and Massachusetts. The Rain Dancer was named for a sloop (a one-masted sailboat) owned by Grassfield. Located at 3031 East Commercial Boulevard, the restaurant was basically a steak operation. The menu featured fourteen meat items and six seafood items that were augmented by a do-it-yourself salad bar. The steaks were placed in a display case just in front of the restaurant's open hearth. The food was cooked exactly to order among lovely surroundings and with friendly and efficient service. The menu was printed on a facsimile breadboard.

From 1972 to 1975, the Rain Dancer was the monthly meeting place (on every third Tuesday) of the Tropical Sports Car Club. The club was dedicated to competitive auto sports, with South Florida rallying being its specialty. The club hosted a beginners' rally school and rallied at the Rain Dancer occasionally.

By 1979, Wayne d'Amato was the restaurant's owner and operator, and for many years, he hosted the annual March of Dimes Holiday Charity

Advertisement highlighting the "Best Steak Award" for the Rain Dancer, 1984. *Courtesy of the* Fort Lauderdale News and Sun-Sentinel.

Dinner. He donated the food and service costs. The Rain Dancer was then sold to Peter and Richard Azzolina in July 1991. The Rain Dancer remained open until circa 2002; at that time, it became Andre's. In 2009, Andre's was put up for auction. Today, the site is a parking lot.

15

Combos

SEA HORSE

Originally opened as Chick Endor and Charlie Farrell's Coral Club on December 21, 1937, the Sea Horse Restaurant was a Fort Lauderdale institution for nearly forty years. It was frequently mentioned in the society pages of the *Fort Lauderdale News* as a setting for wedding receptions, art and fashion shows and Junior Service League charity events. Located at 900 East Las Olas Boulevard, the building was designed in the New Orleans French style by Russell T. Pancoast (a prominent Miami Beach architect). Endor and Farrell were internationally known entertainers, and the Coral Club was called "the smartest new restaurant in Florida." However, entertainers don't always make the best restaurateurs, and by early 1941, the club was failing.

Known for a short time as the Embassy Club, the Sea Horse was opened on November 22, 1941, with new owners. Albert W. Erkins, M.A. Hortt and B. Tippins Jr. Erkins and Hortt were realtors and land developers, and they helped shape Fort Lauderdale in the 1920s and 1930s. Beginning on January 1, 1943, Erkins and Hortt leased the restaurant to Robert Yates, Chester Good and Vincent Millerick. A 1944 advertisement promoted it as "a dining place of distinction."

In November 1945, Sam Harris purchased the Sea Horse. Harris, an immigrant from Crete, was the former owner of the Stage Door Café in Detroit, Michigan, and the Stage Door in Miami Beach. After it was renovated, the restaurant had a main dining room, a dining and dance

The Sea Horse Restaurant on Las Olas Boulevard, 1950s. *Author's collection.*

patio and a theater cocktail lounge. Its menu featured seafood (oysters, lobster, clams, scallops, shrimp and pompano), steaks (sirloin, filet mignon and T-bone) and lamb and pork chops. In April 1950, Harris was elected as the first president of the new Fort Lauderdale Restaurant Association. Beginning in 1952, new seafood and charcoal-broiled specialties (Maine lobster, frog legs, swordfish steak, prime rib roast and roast duckling) were added to the menu.

A 1954 *Fort Lauderdale News* advertisement remarked, "The food has long been known as of top quality in this mid-boulevard spot, the beef is always 'prime.' Known as 'The Well of the Seas,' Maine lobster, green turtle soup, pompano and other sea food favorites are featured here." By 1953, Harris was operating the Sea Horse, the Town House and the Bahia Mar Yacht Club. In 1954, Harris leased the Sea Horse to Fred Wenner.

Wenner turned the Sea Horse into one of the town's most popular luncheon and dinner spots. During his ten-year run, Wenner closed the restaurant for the summer (until then, the restaurant had been open year-round); he also instituted a daily feature that was so successful that his customers came to look forward to certain specials on certain days. As much as he wanted to change them, Wenner stated that his customers associated the days with the items, so switching them wasn't possible. He also introduced his famous dessert: brandy snapps. In 1964, Wenner left the Sea Horse to open his own restaurant.

Sam Harris once again took control of the restaurant after Wenner left, and he completely remodeled the building with a new colonial front and new interior décor. The Sea Horse's marine décor was replaced with deep reds and dark-paneled walls with arched partitions. Harris reopened the restaurant during the summer months and initiating Sunday closings. New seafood offerings (finnan haddie, shad roe, lobster newberg, shrimp creole) were introduced to the menu along with a new fondue sandwich (corned beef and melted swiss cheese on rye). Harris passed in March 1967, but his family continued operating the Sea Horse until 1969.

Chris Wagner and George E. Becker took over the operation of the Sea Horse on November 9, 1970. Wagner ran the restaurant from November 1972 to 1980, except for three years when it was leased to other managers. While carefully preserving the traditions and popular menu items that made the Sea Horse famous, Wagner introduced a vastly expanded menu that included economical daily specials, scrumptious pastries, "the best sandwiches in town," excellent steaks and seafood.

The Sea Horse remained open until 1980. It was then purchased by John "Jack" Boyle, who renovated the building and renamed it Poet's. In 1992, the restaurant was bought by John Day, and it became Mango's. As of February 2019, Piazza Italia occupies the site.

SIERRA INN

Opened in July 1955 at 1221 North Federal Highway, the Sierra Inn was owned and operated by Chris Wagner. Wagner had previously owned the Bamboo Shack on Northeast Ninth Street. The Sierra Inn offered a large and varied menu with extremely reasonable prices. Its menu items included lobster, filet mignon, southern fried chicken and roast prime ribs of beef. In 1956, a Friday night special was introduced: broiled Florida lobster, all you can eat for $1.95. Later, an all-you-can-eat filet mignon special (also $1.95) and an all-you-can-eat southern fried chicken special were added. All of the restaurant's specials came with all-you-can-eat soup, potatoes, coleslaw and hot rolls with butter.

In 1962, Wagner sold the Sierra Inn to Ray and Betty Leary. Interestingly, Wagner had sold the Bamboo Shack to John and Mary Leary (no relation). Wagner was selling so that he could concentrate on his new venture, the Seven Pillars restaurant. The Learys expanded the menu and redecorated

Exterior of the Sierra Inn, which featured "All You Can Eat" specials. *Author's collection.*

the dining room (the American Room) with copies of famous historical documents on the walls. Wagner regained control of the Sierra Inn in 1966, and he sold it again, in 1968, to Harry Calevas. Calevas renovated the restaurant by splitting the large dining room into two, installing an ice cream fountain and updating the menu to include venison, buffalo, pheasant and escargot. The days of the $1.99 all-you-can-eat gimmick were done. In August 1970, a smorgasbord buffet was added.

By 1972, Calevas had gone into the modular fast food business in Texas; he had invented and patented a self-contained unit that could be placed at a site (like a gas station) and be providing hot food service within twenty-four hours. Gerry Kreiser was the owner of the Sierra Inn by 1972, and Tony Nick operated it in 1973 and 1974, when it closed. Between 1975 and 1984, when the building shuttered for good, it was variously known as the Peking Restaurant, the Castle of the Sea, the Captain's Wheel, Paprika, Maggie Mae's, Square One, Horsetooth Reservoir, the New Gateway Lounge and the Sicily Inn. Today, the Sunrise Square Shopping Center is located at the site.

SEVEN PILLARS

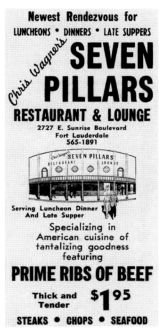

Newest Rendezvous for
LUNCHEONS • DINNERS • LATE SUPPERS

Chris Wagner's
SEVEN PILLARS
RESTAURANT & LOUNGE
2727 E. Sunrise Boulevard
Fort Lauderdale
565-1891

Serving Luncheon Dinner
And Late Supper

Specializing in
American cuisine of
tantalizing goodness
featuring
PRIME RIBS OF BEEF

Thick and $**1**95
Tender

STEAKS • CHOPS • SEAFOOD

Opening month advertisement, 1962. *Courtesy of the* Fort Lauderdale News.

On December 9, 1962, at 2727 East Sunrise Boulevard, Chris Wagner's Seven Pillars Restaurant was opened, ushering in the launch of the new Sunrise Bay Shopping Center. Featuring a pillared Monticello-like façade, the 270-seat restaurant showcased authentic early American décor that included a carpet that was a copy of the one that was presented to Martha Washington by the Marquis de Lafayette. The restaurant's Moby Dick Lounge was decorated with bas-relief scenes of whaling and the New England sea.

Specializing in American cuisine, the Seven Pillars served choice steaks, chops, poultry and seafood. It baked its own bread and pastries, and it served roast prime rib of beef, Virginian ham, beef ribs, pot roast, roast leg of lamb, lobster, shrimp, and crab. A 1962 advertisement for the opening of the restaurant touted that it had the "finest food, prepared to perfection in [its] new clean, modern all-electric kitchen." The restaurant's specialty was an open-face hot turkey sandwich with supreme sauce that was run under the broiler to melt a hefty serving of cheese. In December 1966, the Seven Pillars introduced a relish gallery.

Wagner operated the Seven Pillars until May 1969, when he sold it to the Longchamps restaurant chain. That October, it became a Steak and Brew and remained open as such until 1975. From 1976 to 1986, the building housed Beefsteak Charlie's. Wagner took over the operation of the Sea Horse Restaurant in late 1970. The old Seven Pillars site is now home to the Sunrise Harbor Luxury apartments complex.

FRED WENNER'S

Fred Wenner grew up in Frankfurt-am-Main, Germany, and came to America in the late 1920s. A former law student, he soon became interested in the food industry. Wenner worked at Coney Island and, later, on Manhattan's East Side. He came to Florida in 1932, and he operated the food concession at the Blackstone Hotel in Miami Beach until 1938. For the next fifteen years, he was a partner at the Gray's Inn Hotel and Restaurant in New Hampshire and Miami Beach. In 1953, Wenner purchased the Sea Horse Restaurant on Las Olas Boulevard, and he turned it into one of the town's most popular luncheon and dinner spots. He operated the restaurant until 1963. At that time, Wenner decided to build and open a new place.

Located at 2525 North Federal Highway, Fred Wenner's was opened on November 11, 1964. When asked why he opened the restaurant, he replied, "Mainly, because I had never built my own place, and I wanted to put all my experiences into a restaurant—from the foundation up." Fred Wenner's was a New Orleans–style restaurant that overlooked the Middle River. It featured thirty-five delicious menu items, including roast prime rib, prime sirloin steaks, filet mignon, red snapper, bay scallops, curried shrimp and oyster on the half shell. The restaurant's pièce de résistance was its frozen brandy snapps. There was no entertainment space in the new restaurant—a departure from the norms of the day in Fort Lauderdale—food was the most

Exterior of Fred Wenner's Restaurant, which operated for six years (1964–70) before becoming a New England Oyster House. *Author's collection.*

important thing to Wenner. "I'm just not an entertainment type. I've tried it but preparing food and serving good food is enough for one man to handle."

Wenner ran the restaurant until October 1968, when he sold it to John and Edward Powell. Wenner stayed on as a food consultant at the restaurant until he retired in 1970. New England Oyster House later bought the restaurant and reopened it under its own name in late July 1970. Over the years, the site has been home to Hacienda del Rio (April 1975 to March 1980), Gepetto's Tale o' the Whale (July 1980 to April 1982) and Costa Brava (July 1982 to December 1984). Since March 1985, it has been home to a Ruth's Chris Steak House.

THE CAVES

The son of Sam's Subway Restaurants founder, Samuel Hochman, and later partner in the chain, Saul Hochman and his wife, Jacquie, left Indianapolis, Indiana, for Fort Lauderdale in 1975. Here, they opened the Caves restaurant,

which was modeled after their former restaurant, the Caves 'N' Caverns, at Northview Mall in Indianapolis. The Caves was located at 2205 North Federal Highway, between Oakland Park and Sunrise Boulevards (the site of the former Tale o' the Tiger). Imitating a journey to prehistoric days, the Caves boasted Stone Age décor and hearty feasting; stalactites hung overhead, and the walls featured Paleolithic sketches. Customers were seated in cave-like cubicles with tanned hide table coverings, and they were served by waitresses in animal-skin-print dresses. The restaurant's menus were printed on a chamois with wooden frames. As a postcard stated, "Enter another world in your own private cave, replete with luxurious pillows and soft lighting." The restaurant's featured

The Caves provided patrons with a prehistoric dining experience for twenty-five years. *Author's collection.*

meals included fresh seafood, steaks and barbecue ribs, complemented by the elegant Silver Salad Bar. The Caves remained open until 2000; its owner and operator, Saul Hochman, passed away in 2003. Today, the Vitamin Shoppe occupies the site.

MR. LAFF'S

For nearly sixteen years, one of Fort Lauderdale's most enduring restaurants and nightclubs was Mr. Laff's, which was located at 1135 North Federal Highway. During the 1940s and 1950s, the property was originally home to the Gateway Motel. In the 1960s, it housed the Town and Country Motel. In 1971, local air-conditioning contractor Clint Ramsden (Engineer Air Corps) purchased the property and decided to turn the main building (where the office and breakfast shop were located) into a more formal restaurant.

While he was undecided on the restaurant's theme and design, Ramsden was approached by nightclub owner and restaurateur Bobby Van (Vannuchi) in late 1972 about becoming partners in an upscale restaurant and nightclub. Van had owned the Jet Set and Bachelors III in Manhattan, New York, and was the owner of Bachelors III in Fort Lauderdale. Ramsden agreed, and they set out to develop Mr. Laff's. "Bobby designed the lounge area, and I handled the construction and finding a kitchen and bar staff," Ramsden recalled. "I was a regular at the Ambry, and I heard it was changing hands and letting everyone go. So, that's where I got most of the original floor staff and great cooks, like Joey Durkin; Tom and his brother, Chuck Weber; Tommy Flynn; and Lloyd Kurak." Mr. Laff's was known for its fine meals and excellent service.

After opening in late September 1976, the place was an instant smash. With the ability to seat seventy-five and a three-bar lounge, Mr. Laff's attracted celebrities, including Van's friend and business partner Joe Namath. A 1980 *Fort Lauderdale News* restaurant listing described it as "good for a luncheon salad bar and soup combination, and for prime rib, chicken teriyaki, stuffed shrimp, fish of the day for dinner." While it was mainly a steak and seafood joint, King Crab was very popular. "If you ask me what our biggest seller was, it was king crab," Ramsden reminisced. "On Sunday and Monday nights, we did an all-you-can-eat king crab special for $7.95, which was a steep price for back then. We

"Catch of the Day" advertisement, 1984. *Courtesy of the* Sun-Sentinel.

couldn't keep enough on hand to serve everyone, because the place was packed. Even though we only broke even on the king crab, we more than made up for it at the bar."

During the off season, the motel was pretty quiet, and Van and Ramsden came up with an idea to bring in daytime business. Van contacted the Miami Dolphins and convinced Joe Robbie that the rookies and free agents who were trying out for the team could stay at the motel for free if they behaved and hung out at the swimming pool and lounge during the week. Paul Lorenzo, the pool bartender, recalled, "Every afternoon, the pool area was packed with girls wanting to meet the players and also with outside guys trying to meet the girls. I made huge money there!" Mr. Laff's maintained a good relationship with the Dolphins for many years. Monday nights from 8:00 to 9:00 p.m. were Dolphin nights, where Henry Barrow of WIOD radio and former safety Mike Kozlowski hosted a live sports talk show on cable television called *South Florida Sports*. Former and current Miami Dolphins were featured guests on the show; other local and national sports figures, celebrities and Dolphin cheerleaders also made appearances.

The Laff's Landing shopping center plaza was built in 1987, with Mr. Laff's as the anchor. The plaza still stands today, but the building is now an AT&T store. Mr. Laff's closed in early 1992, and it later became Collage Night Club, Napa Grill, Aladdin Café and Arena Sports Bar.

BURT AND JACK'S

Originally opened in 1979 at Berth 23 in Port Everglades, Burt and Jack's Spanish mission–style building previously housed Luminarias, which was owned by the Specialty Restaurant Corporation, Normandy Beach (with a World War II theme) and Pleasures. Actor Burt Reynolds partnered with restaurateur Leon "Jack" Jackson after flying over the property in October 1983 during the filming of the movie *Stick*. Jackson was developing the property, and Reynolds contacted him to see if he would be interested in partnering. The pair met at Reynolds's home in Jupiter, Florida, and Jackson agreed.

The 250-seat restaurant was housed in a charming, Spanish-style villa; it featured fine food and service, waterfront views, tropical gardens and a strict dress code (jackets required). New York strip steaks, huge lobsters, fresh local seafood and gigantic desserts were the restaurant's specialties. It was the first major USDA prime steakhouse in Fort Lauderdale and was famous for its baked, stuffed lobster. "Burt and I agreed that everything was to be top-notch," recalled Jackson. One local food critic "likened dinner at Burt and Jack's to dining on a luxury cruise ship." The restaurant was a popular gathering spot for sports and entertainment personalities, and it was the site of many charity events, weddings and anniversaries. Reynolds also dropped by to have dinner occasionally. Penne Auger Thompson commented, "One of the best in South Florida. Great food, beautiful ambiance, and you never knew who might be dining there with you!"

Burt and Jack's launch party was held on May 19, 1984, at Port Everglades. It was a celebrity-filled event—minus movie star and copartner Burt Reynolds, who was laid up with kidney stones at the Pier 66 Hotel. The star-studded premiere was attended by about thirty of Reynolds's Hollywood friends, including Ricardo Montalbán, Esther Williams, Dom DeLuise, Charles Nelson Reilly, George Segal, Ernest Borgnine and his then-girlfriend, Loni Anderson, who had flown in for the event. Local celebrity H. Wayne Huizenga and new Miami Dolphins quarterback Dan Marino also attended. The event was the first date of Marino and Claire Veazey, his future wife. The restaurant was also where, in 1990, WSHE radio executives met to discuss the possible paring of DJs Ron Brewer and Paul Castronovo. Paul and Ron's banter had the table in stitches, and they were given a morning show. This led to a twenty-six-year-long on-air partnership.

Burt and Jack's remained open for eighteen years and closed in June 2002, due to the stifling security measures that were put in place at the port

Burt Reynolds, restaurateur Jack Jackson (*right*) and Kathy Jackson (*center*) at the fifth anniversary celebration of Burt and Jack's restaurant at Port Everglades in June 1989. *Courtesy of the* Sun-Sentinel.

following the 9/11 terrorist attacks. The restaurant's patronage dropped, as diners had to pass through checkpoints and show identification just to get there. The building was demolished in 2006, and it is now a restricted dock. Jack Jackson went on to be the longtime owner of Jackson's Steakhouse on Las Olas Boulevard, which closed in 2009. He later opened Fish, a high-end seafood place, and Jackson's Bar and Grill to little success. In 2017, Jackson opened Jackson's Prime on Galt Ocean Mile.

PART 3

DINERS, DRIVE-INS AND BARBECUE

Bring me four fried chickens and a Coke.
—*Joliet Jake Blues*

Cheeseburger, cheeseburger, cheeseburger. Four Pepsi, two chips.
—Saturday Night Live *skit*

Like much of America in the 1950s, Fort Lauderdale developed the diners, drive-ins and barbecue joints that became public meeting places as people began leaving their traditional family centers and being able to move around after the rise of the personal automobile. Local diners, cafés and cafeterias located themselves near the shopping centers and entertainment areas to cater to local shoppers and leisure seekers. Places like the Day-Lite Café, the Holiday Diner, Mutt and Jeff's Café and Morrison's Cafeteria accommodated these shoppers. The Rainbow Restaurant was located opposite the Florida and Warnor movie theaters on Las Olas Boulevard.

The rise of car culture in the 1950s also had an impact on the Fort Lauderdale restaurant scene, especially when it came to drive-ins. The weekend cruising circuit in Fort Lauderdale started on Sunrise Boulevard; it looped south on Federal Highway, to the Seventeenth Street Causeway, then headed east, to the beach, and then it moved north, along the beach on A1A, until it arrived back at Sunrise Boulevard. Jerry's Drive-In (and, later, Neba's Roast Beef) was the northern hub of the circuit, where guys could show off their cars. Pizio's Drive-Inn was generally the southern stop. Mayer's, Diney's,

The Riptide restaurant, located at 1309 South Federal Highway. Originally with open-air seating, it was eventually enclosed. Today, a Holy Cross Medical Group office is located there. *Author's collection.*

Palmer's and Jimmie's were other popular drive-ins. The A&W was also very popular, as it was located across the street from Fort Lauderdale High School, near downtown.

Barbecue joints have always been popular in Fort Lauderdale. Roscoe's Quick Service Bar-B-Que, the Humpty Dumpty Barbecue and Brady's Barbecue served all kinds of tasty morsels. The Original Bar-B-Que Pit, which was located on south Federal Highway, near the airport, was regarded as the best barbecue joint in town. It featured picnic tables and a screened in dining area. Its famous patrons included Danny Kaye, Buddy Hackett and Dr. Joyce Brothers.

16

Diners

BROWN'S GOOD FOOD

Native Nebraskan and traveling salesman Logan T. Brown came to Fort Lauderdale in 1925. He was initially involved with real estate and sold a soda shop called the Soda Smoke to a coast guard officer, who had purchased it for his wife to run. After the bust and depression that followed the 1926 hurricane, the couple wanted out, and Brown took the shop back. With no new takers and with real estate sales at a standstill, Brown proceeded to run the Soda Smoke alongside his wife. Located in the old McCrory's building on South Andrews Avenue, the Soda Smoke began serving hot meals and soon grew out of its location.

Brown then moved the restaurant into the Bryan Arcade, at the corner of Andrews Avenue and Southwest Second Street, renamed it Brown's Good Food and expanded the menu. "I remember all the bad meals I ate in restaurants on the road," Brown once said. "I try to give people what I always hoped I might get when I went into a strange restaurant." The restaurant's special Sunday dinners were advertised as costing anywhere from fifty cents to one dollar. His tactic worked so well that, during the winter season, the lines outside his restaurant were several blocks long. In 1940, after six years in the Bryan Arcade, Brown bought property around the corner, 229 Brickell Avenue, and built a restaurant that could seat 250 people.

The new building was considered an addition to the architectural beauty of the city. Brown's Good Food was one of downtown Fort Lauderdale's most important establishments. It was famous for its "pot roast table," a

Brown's Good Food's second location in the Bryan Arcade, on the corner of Andrews Avenue and Southwest Second Street. *Courtesy of the Broward County Historical Archives, Broward County Library.*

gathering place for the city's power brokers. Every day, the male community leaders joined each other for lunch in a group that consisted of judges, lawyers, bankers, doctors and businessmen. There, the men exchanged jokes and opinions on a wide variety of topics around a table that could sit twenty. There was no restriction on who could sit there, but no stranger would dare intrude, and no politician could fail to make an appearance come campaign season. The pot roast table attendees, who shared this table from the mid-1920s to the late 1950s, comprised much of the power and wealth of Fort Lauderdale, and most of them left their mark in the city's history. Attorney George English once recalled, "It was completely informal—just good fellowship. About the only requirements were that you be an adult male and really be able to take it, because believe me, we really dished it out."

Logan Brown was honored in 1952 as Florida's outstanding restaurateur by the Florida Restaurant Association. In 1960, Brown's Good Food was sold to Otto Horacek of Chicago. While maintaining that "the food [would] be the same, cooked by Mr. Brown's own staff," the restaurant was not the same and closed after about a year and a half. When he retired, Brown stated, "I couldn't have done this without 'Stuckey.'" Homer Stuckey was a thirty-four-year employee who began working for Brown for free during the bust of 1926. After closing, Brown's Good Food was replaced with Thompson's Business Supply Store. Logan Brown passed away in 1962.

HINKLE'S CAFÉ

George Hinkle, a Michigan native, arrived in Fort Lauderdale in 1923. He opened his first restaurant (Hinkle's Lunch Room) on Wall Street in 1929 (located where the 4 West Las Olas apartment and retail complex is currently being built). Renamed Hinkle's Café, his restaurant remained at this location until the 1939–40 winter season. Its advertisements from the 1930s stated that it was the "home of home-cooked foods" and that it would "be happy to meet all of our old friends as well as new ones." Hinkle was elected the first secretary of the newly formed Broward Restaurant Association in August 1933.

During the 1939–40 season, Hinkle's Café moved around the corner to 216 Southwest First (Brickell) Avenue (now the AutoNation Building). Advertisements during the early 1940s proclaimed, "Enjoy a perfectly prepared tasty meal, in a cool, comfortable, friendly café, where food and service are better." The restaurant was "where every meal [was] a memory." On November 10, 1942, the café hosted a luncheon for the Forty-Fifth District Convention of District Four of the Florida Woodmen Circle.

By October 1944, Hinkle's Café had once again relocated to 411 South Andrews Avenue, just south of the New River (currently an empty lot). By then, the restaurant was serving breakfast, lunch and dinner six days a week (it was closed on Sundays). During the 1949 Andrews Avenue Bridge

Interior view of Hinkle's Café. *Courtesy of the State Archives of Florida, Florida Memory.*

replacement, in which the crossing was closed for ten months, George Hinkle stated in a January 24 *Fort Lauderdale Daily News* article that "he [was] losing $30 a day because of the rerouting of traffic." He did, however, supply a twenty-dollar meal ticket as a giveaway at the bridge-opening celebration.

At the time of George Hinkle's unexpected death, in January 1952, the café had again moved to 1413 South Andrews Avenue (now the parking lot of Tap 42 Bar and Kitchen). By October 1952, the café was operating at 219 Southwest First (Brickell) Avenue, "serving Mrs. Hinkle's well-known homemade pies." A February 1954 notice stated that the café was up for auction as an "established year-round restaurant business that grosses from $80–$100 per day." City directories contain no listings for Hinkle's after 1955.

17

Drive-Ins

DOUMAR'S DRIVE-IN

The invention of the ice cream cone led to the opening of the "nation's most unusual drive-in restaurant," Doumar's, at 3001 North Federal Highway in 1951. The joint venture between brothers Joseph and Edward Doumar followed the family's tradition of participating in food service. The brothers' father, Abraham Doumar, was a Lebanese immigrant from Damascus, Syria, who was a salesman at the 1904 St. Louis World's Fair (Louisiana Purchase Exposition). On either side of his booth were an ice cream vendor and a waffle maker. One night, Abraham rolled up a waffle and filled it with ice cream. He spent the rest of the fair selling the world's first ice cream cones.

In 1905, Abraham opened a chain of ice cream stands that eventually stretched from Coney Island, New York, to Jacksonville, Florida. His stand at Ocean View Amusement Park in Norfolk, Virginia, was his most successful, and he turned the operation of it over to his brother, George. George relocated the stand to Monticello Avenue in Norfolk after the 1933 hurricane, and he expanded it into a full-service drive-in, which is still open today.

Following Abraham's death in 1946, the Doumar sons moved to Detroit before eventually settling in Fort Lauderdale in 1951. Joseph and Edward opened the city's first drive-in restaurant, which quickly became one of its most popular destinations for food and fun. Known for its mid-century modern design and unique waterfall design concept, patrons could dine

The mid-century modern Doumar's was Fort Lauderdale's first drive-in. *Author's collection.*

in the drive-in's colorful dining room or in the privacy of their own cars among the palm trees and falling water of the "flying saucers." Doumar's received several national architectural awards. The drive-in remained open until 1962. Joseph later opened his own liquor store and became a real estate dealer. Edward later opened the Alley Cat Lounge. The Ramada Oakland Park Inn now sits at the former site of Doumar's.

PIZIO'S DRIVE-INN

Pizio's Drive-Inn had its grand opening in Fort Lauderdale on April 16, 1953. Situated at 1505 South Federal Highway, Pizio's was just one of ten locations owned and operated by the Pizio brothers. Pizio's original location was opened in 1939 in Syracuse, New York, by brothers Albert and James Pizio. Two other brothers operated the Florida branches. The Fort Lauderdale site was the second location in Florida (the location in Dania was the first). Pizio's even had a location in Cuba before it was confiscated by Fidel Castro.

James Pizio and Arthur Hammond came to Fort Lauderdale in 1950 to assist in the construction of Pizio's Drive-Inns. Mario Pizio became the

Grand opening advertisement from April 16, 1953. *Courtesy of the* Fort Lauderdale Daily News.

owner and manager of the Fort Lauderdale location in 1955 (the restaurant was located at the former site of the Red Fox). Selling "good food at sensible prices" was Pizio's mission. Pizio's Drive-Inn was known for its pizza, spaghetti and large Italian sandwiches. Its specialty was the giant hoagy sandwich ("a meal in a loaf of bread").

Every effort was made by the restaurant to provide an intimate and friendly atmosphere. The parking lot accommodated seventy-five automobiles for those who wished to be served by the restaurant's courteous and efficient carhops. Initially open 24/7, Pizio's had to curb its hours following noise complaints by neighboring businesses (mainly hotels and apartment complexes). Lou Ming recalled, "I used to go there with Mom and Dad and my brother. They had car service, and we'd get foot-long hot dogs. Yum!" Susan Lopez Moore concurred, "I have been around the world three times, and I swear, to me, this was the best pizza I ever had—boy would I love a slice." Around 1974, all of the Florida Pizio's Drive-Inns closed. The Fort Lauderdale location became the Key West Seafood House, which operated until 1989. Today, the site houses the Rio Vista Shopping Plaza.

JERRY'S DRIVE-IN

Jerry's Drive-In was part of a chain of restaurants that was founded by Jerome Mitchell Lederer of Lexington, Kentucky. Lederer opened a chain of restaurants in Lexington before founding the Jerry's chain in 1946. Eventually, he operated forty-one Jerry's Drive-Ins in seven states. In 1957, Lederer moved to Fort Lauderdale, bought the Big Joy Drive-In at 1624

Jerry's DRIVE-IN RESTAURANT

Just As Near As Your Phone

LEXINGTON (4)

WINCHESTER

DANVILLE

FRANKFORT

SHELBYVILLE

LOUISVILLE (3)

BOWLING GREEN

OWENSBORO

NEW ALBANY, IND.

FORT LAUDERDALE, FLA.

Golden Fried Chicken

⅓ Golden Fried Chicken
with Tangy Cole Slaw
Idaho French Fried
Potatoes and Hot Rolls
$1.00

- Dining Room Service
- Car Service
- Carry Out Service

Advertisement in the *Wildcat Tip-Off: Kentucky vs. Alabama February 23, 1959* basketball program. *Courtesy of the Kentucky Digital Library.*

East Sunrise Boulevard and reopened it as a Jerry's. According to Lederer, Jimmie Foxx, the major-league baseball player and the then-head coach of the University of Miami baseball team, helped select the place. The restaurant remained open until 1967. Cyndi Barnett was a carhop at Jerry's in 1965; she said that the restaurant had the "best hamburgers around!"

Jerry's Drive-In was the place to be seen during the 1960s. "Jerry's was the place to cruise to on Friday and Saturday nights," said David Potter. Lee Gerali said, "[I] hung out there thru high school. Everyone drove through so they could be seen in their cool cars. Loved it!" Even local football legend and former Chicago Bears fullback Brian Piccolo would cruise A1A in his 1957 Chevy and hang out with his friends at Jerry's Drive-In.

After Jerry's closed, the custom car cruisers relocated six blocks east on Sunrise Boulevard, to Neba's Roast Beef. Over the next decade, the Jerry's site was home to Ray's Drive-In, the Portico Restaurant, Frederic's Seven Flags, Stuarts of London, Big Bar and Restaurant and Bubba's. The Elan 16Forty apartment complex is currently located on the site.

NEBA ROAST BEEF

Founded by Michael Davis in Albany, New York, in the early 1960s, the Neba Roast Beef chain was the first to enter the roast beef sandwich market. It eventually moved its corporate headquarters to Hollywood, Florida, and by 1969, there were seventy locations in operation. Though its name was thought to be an acronym for "never eat burgers again" or "never eat beef at Arby's," and despite the later use of the advertising slogan "nicest eating beef around," the chain was, in fact, named after a dog that Davis had owned.

In 1967, George Foerst, an owner of three eating establishments in Pennsylvania, came to Florida for winter vacation and decided to never go back. He became a franchisee for Neba in 1968 and opened one of the first two Nebas in Florida, which was located at the intersection of North Federal Highway and Sunrise Boulevard (1100 North Federal), across from the Gateway Shopping Center. During its eighteen years in operation, Foerst estimated that it sold over 6 million juicy, thinly sliced, top-round roast beef sandwiches (1.5 million pounds of beef). The tater tots and black cow milkshakes were also favorites of the restaurant's patrons.

The Neba chain declared bankruptcy in 1970, due to competition from Arby's, but Foerst continued to operate his location until 1986 (it is currently a PNC Bank). He had sold the property in 1978 and operated it on a month-to-month lease. In the end, Nebas of Fort Lauderdale had more than two

One of the first Neba's in Florida, in the Gateway Area of Fort Lauderdale, 1968. *Courtesy of the* Fort Lauderdale News and Sun-Sentinel.

hundred regular customers, including dentist Thomas Rypavy, who stopped by daily for a Super Neba and a large Coke.

Neba's vivid yellow façade was a beacon for owners of classic custom cars; the restaurant was popular not only for its roast beef sandwiches but also for its central location and large parking area. It became a Saturday night hangout, where car enthusiasts could show off their hot rods after Jerry's Drive-In closed (approximately six blocks to the west). *Car Craft* magazine once called Neba the "hottest spot in America on a Saturday night." Foerst lamented the fact that the flashy cars generally got more publicity than his sandwiches. "In all the advertisements we had, no one ever talked about the roast beef." After getting out of the restaurant business, Foerst started Awnings Inc. of Broward with his son, George Jr. The pair provided commercial awnings and had major accounts with Taco Bell and McDonald's.

18

Barbecue

JOE'S BAR-B-Q AND JOE'S RESTAURANT

This establishment has ties with Fort Lauderdale that date back to 1923. That year, Harris Joseph Hudson and his new bride, Lucille, arrived in the city from Nashville, Tennessee, and opened a grocery store downtown (on the corner of Brickell Avenue and Southwest Second Street). This store was damaged in the 1926 hurricane. Discouraged, the Hudsons returned to Nashville but came back the following year. In 1929, they opened Joe's Bar-B-Q at 600 East Las Olas Boulevard (where the Cheesecake Factory and the Riverside Hotel Executive Tower stand today). The stone-faced building and adjoining G.M. Wall Texaco station sat on the southeast corner of Las Olas Boulevard and Federal Highway.

The couple's booming business lured people from as far away as Palm Beach; they just wanted to get a taste of the restaurant's chili and barbecue. The place was an immediate hit. Joe and Lucy sold hamburgers for a dime, barbecue and chili for twenty cents, Cokes for a nickel and big plates of beef stew for a quarter. "They had the best hamburgers in town," said former mayor Virginia Young. Poet Edgar A. Guest enjoyed the place so much that he wrote two poems ("Joe's" and "Return to Joe's") about it.

> *There, Joe and Miss Lucy attend us*
> *With care that's heart-warming to find.*
> *We know they'd be quick to befriend us,*

They're gentle and gracious and kind.
Oh, none is too proud to be seen there,
It's a spot to which everyone goes;
And happy I am to have been there
And share in the welcome to Joe's

—*fourth stanza of "Joe's," by Edgar A. Guest*

Chili was popular among the moonshine drinkers from the town's illegal stills; the chili grease lined their stomachs and prevented gastritis. Fort Lauderdale High School (which was located one block north of Joe's) students also provided the restaurant with a good deal of business. "Joe knew most of the kids by their first names," recalled Harry Spyke. Joe's was also a popular hangout spot for the local police. Sara Crim remembered, "The police always went there for their coffee." The restaurant was very successful, and Joe invested his profits wisely; he opened the Sun and Sand Beach Hotel in 1946 (with his brother-in-law, Douglas Lockhart, of city commission and stadium fame), he owned a laundromat and he opened Hudson's Arcade (a strip of shops and restaurants) just north of Las Olas Boulevard on A1A.

Joe's Bar-B-Q and the G.M. Wall Texaco station were located on the southeast corner of Las Olas Boulevard and Federal Highway, late 1930s. *Courtesy of History Fort Lauderdale.*

In 1958, the city decided to build a tunnel under the New River to relieve traffic jams from the Federal Highway drawbridge. Due to the construction, Joe felt that it time to retire and closed the restaurant that May. Shortly after closing the business, Hudson sold it to George E. Gilbert ,who reopened it just two months later at 525 West Sunrise Boulevard. Gilbert kept the name in honor of Joe Hudson. Gilbert ran the place until 1990, when he sold it. The restaurant finally closed in 2004.

KIM'S CABIN

William (Bill) Kimmerling came to Fort Lauderdale from Roanoke, Virginia, in 1933. After working as a manager at Family Loan Company and owning Kim's Motor Sales, Bill and his brother, Louis, opened Kim's Package Liquor Store in 1948. It was the first business in the Gateway Shopping Center. By 1952, they had converted the store into a full-service bar. The Kimmerlings sold Kim's Alley Bar to Tom McAdams in 1959. Bill Kimmerling then opened Kim's Cabin restaurant at 321 West Sunrise Boulevard in 1956.

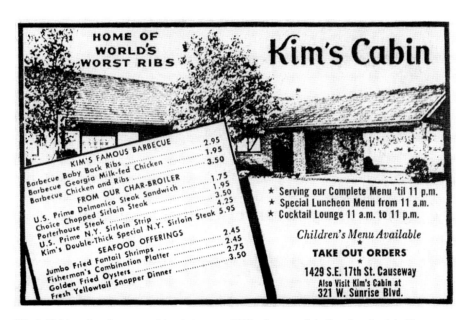

Kim's Cabin advertisement with mini menu, 1969. *Courtesy of the* Fort Lauderdale News.

Specializing in baby back ribs from Iowa, the restaurant's original menu was compact, with only barbecued ribs or chicken and a combination platter. The restaurant later added steak, steak sandwiches and other barbecue sandwiches. Kim's Cabin was a popular lunch and dinner spot. Billing itself as the "home of the world's worst ribs," Kim's Cabin's menus featured the phrase, "Preparation of good food takes time…yours will be ready in a minute." The ribs were good, and the restaurant had a friendly, homey, family-style atmosphere. In February 1967, Kimmerling opened a second Kim's Cabin location at 1492 Southeast Seventeenth Street Causeway. A near replica of the Sunrise Boulevard location, it featured the same menu items but added seafood offerings (lobster and oysters).

Both locations operated until the mid-1970s. Kim's Sunrise Cabin was sold to Joe Erma and Wynn Donnelly in 1973; by August 1975, it had been replaced with Prelude, a New York–style supper club. Today, the site is home to 321 Slammer, a private club for gay men. Kim's Causeway Cabin closed in 1974 and reopened as the Ground Round Lounge. Today, the location is a parking lot for the Extended Stay America hotel.

ERNIE'S BAR-B-Q

Opened in 1957 by Ernie Siebert, Ernie's Bar-B-Q (originally known as Dirty Ernie's Bar) was a Fort Lauderdale institution renowned for its conch chowder and world-famous Bimini bread. Located at 1843 South Federal Highway, the restaurant was popular with locals and tourists alike, and it was known for its rooftop patio, live music and quirky libertarian quotes on the walls about the nature of money and the evils of taxation. For years, its menus stated, "Where conch is king, barbecue is a way of life and the bar is open late!"

Siebert was a man of many stories. He was a wheeler-dealer and part-time rumrunner. Local lore says that Siebert once bought $250,000 worth of alcohol and stored it in Bimini. Whenever Ernie's ran low on booze, Siebert would make the trip over to the island by boat and bring back a load to avoid the taxes. In October 1972, Ernie's was raided, and Siebert faced charges of possession of untaxed liquor from the Florida State Beverage Department. According to some locals, the upstairs, open-air patio was a good spot to have a cold drink after work and watch the "working girls" on Federal Highway.

South exterior of Ernie's Bar-B-Q, with main entrance. Home of renowned conch chowder and Bimini bread. *Courtesy of PassageMaker.com.*

The restaurant was later called Ernie's Booze and Bar-B-Q, and the Klawsky family bought it from Siebert in 1976. They operated the restaurant until 1997, when it was sold to Frank "Butch" Samp, who also owned the Floridian Restaurant and Tina's Spaghetti House. "I like to save the old restaurants," said Samp. "I like the history that comes with them. You get fifty years of stories." In March 2017, Ernie's Bar-B-Q closed its doors, triggering outcry from both local and non-local customers. Posts from their Facebook page included:

> *So sad...my family has been going here EVERY YEAR for over 35 years!!!!*
> *My mom drives from Arizona just for this.*
> *—Suzzy Meredith*

> *I have been going to Ernie's my entire life. This is very sad to us Fort Lauderdale natives.*
> *—Matt Norris*

> *I have been eating there since 1969, and I am going to miss the food big time!*
> *—D'Ann Ford.*

Samp sold the property to successful restaurateur Anthony Bruno (Anthony's Runway 84 and Anthony's Cold-Fired Pizza), who reopened it on December 28, 2018, as Andy's Live Fire Grill and Bar.

PART 4

A LITTLE SOMETHING FOR EVERYONE

It all comes back to the basics. Serve customers the best-tasting food at a good value in a clean, comfortable restaurant, and they'll keep coming back.
—*Dave Thomas*

Everyone has their favorite restaurant, and sometimes, the deciding factors of where to dine are ambiance and atmosphere. Fort Lauderdale has had many themed and unique dining places over the years. Many times, the interior decoration of the restaurant has conveyed that theme, but occasionally, the exterior reinforces it too. The buildings were constructed in such a way to draw patrons in and give them an idea of the restaurants' menus and dining environments. Examples of these restaurants include the Red Barn, the Bridge (old

Opened in the early 1980s, the Area Code 305 Restaurant featured a telephone system to make calls to other tables. Powdy the clown and singing waiters would entertain the customers. *Author's collection.*

English atmosphere), the Loft Restaurant and Lounge (with its famous "Work Wagon" salad bar) and the Litchfield Farm House Restaurant ("Home of Broward's best burger"). Other interesting dining establishments in Fort Lauderdale have included the Forum ("Fort Lauderdale's only family-planned restaurant"), the 700 Restaurant on Las Olas Boulevard (late 1930s, "our telephone number, like our name, is 700") and Jack Valentine's Restaurant and Lounge (with ice show).

Aside from Fort Lauderdale's ethnic food choices, its standard surf and turfs and fast-food places, healthy choice eateries have also found their niches. In the 1960s, the Spartan Restaurant served health food, and its motto was "good food is our business—so is your health." Opened in 1978, Nature's Oven was a vegetarian fast-food establishment in Fort Lauderdale.

19
The Deck

The Deck was opened on November 10, 1934, at 330 South Andrews Avenue, and its formal opening was held on Thanksgiving. Located just north of the Andrews Avenue Bridge on the northeast corner of Andrews Avenue and New River Drive, the restaurant was owned by Alfred Parker Crooks and Mr. Larson. Captain (Lord Algy) Crooks was a charter boatman before becoming a barkeep. The Deck served seafood, steaks, chops and chicken prepared by French chef Jean. By January 1935, Crooks was the sole owner, and Mrs. Crooks was personally in charge of the dining room and kitchen.

When the Deck opened for the season in December 1936, it featured specialties of oysters and clams served on the half shell. The clams and oysters were opened on the premises, an innovation for Fort Lauderdale. Frank Sykes, a seafood specialist, was the new chef, and the restaurant's interior featured a marine motif, with blues and greens as the predominant color scheme.

Skipper Fred Beck and his wife, Eva Duncan, came from Englewood, New Jersey, in 1937 and bought the Deck from Alfred Parker Crooks. Crooks had recently opened Club Rendezvous (later Club Alamo) in January 1937 and was focusing his energies there. George Young operated his Chop Suey Parlor at the Deck from June to October 1939. Advertisements in 1940 touted that the Deck served "Chinese, Italian, American food at its best" and that its "charcoal-broiled steaks [were] a

THE DECK
Steaks, Chops, Sea Food, Chinese Food
One of the World's Famous Bars
On New River
Fort Lauderdale, Florida

Skipper
Fred Beck

Cruise Director
Eve Duncan

Postcard showing the exterior, interior and hosts of the Deck. *Courtesy of the State Archives of Florida, Florida Memory.*

specialty." In May 1944, Crooks sold Club Alamo to Beck. He ran it for one year until it closed in 1945. In a February 23, 1945 article, "P's and Q's by Stella," she remarked,

> *What days those at the* DECK, *Fred Beck's cypress paneled horseshoe bar and dining room by the bridge on Andrews Avenue at the River! There, one might encounter the Duke and Duchess of Windsor, Howard Johnson, or any famous Hollywood star stopping midway between Miami and Palm Beach for dinner and amusement at the* DECK. *Times and faces have changed a bit, but the same good pianist tinkles merry tunes to make the evening gay for the dropper-in from four o'clock until curfew. Last evening, I encountered there almost the whole crew of an aircraft carrier just put into port; another evening, it might be filled with Ft. Lauderdalians and winter visitors dining out. Yachting crowd or navy, they all* HIT THE DECK *when in a bohemian mood and enjoy the fun.*

Skipper Beck operated the Deck until 1948. For the 1951–2 season, he managed the Bahia Mar Restaurant, and in 1953, he was operating the Stage Door in Hollywood, Florida. Abel Dewitt (Woodrow) Holmes was the owner of the Deck by 1955, but he was arrested for bookmaking, and the Deck was closed shortly after that. It was reopened by Beck in 1962 as a part of the Broward Hotel. By 1970, Beck was the general manager at Albert Brown Inc. (mutual funds and insurance). Bubier Park now occupies the site.

20
Pal's

Frank "Hank" Hagmann arrived in Fort Lauderdale from Irvington, New Jersey, in 1945. He became the manager of the Boulevard Hotel and La Fiesta Cocktail Lounge in 1946. Hagmann opened Pal's, located at 1745 East Sunrise Boulevard, on November 20, 1947. A *Fort Lauderdale Daily News* advertisement stated:

> *Tomorrow night…you are invited to attend the opening of Fort Lauderdale's most unique…most distinctive…and most intimate restaurant and cocktail lounge. Here at Pal's, under the direction of Hank Hagmann, you will find delicious food and fine drinks served in the friendliest atmosphere in Florida, with a background of ultra-modern decoration by George Lamarche, designer.*

Pal's featured continental and international cuisine, and according to a 1950 *Fort Lauderdale Daily News* advertisement, "With advance notice, Chef George Duke will prepare any foreign dish from any country." In September 1949, Hagmann opened a package (liquor) store that was adjacent to Pal's. Air conditioning was installed at the restaurant in July 1951 to maintain year-round operations. In that same year, Heinz Zimmerman, a pianist, began his long-term residency at Pal's.

During the 1950s, Hagmann expanded his operations, opening a Pal's in Pompano Beach (1955) and Pal's Captain's Table in Deerfield Beach (1957). Starting on August 1, 1961, Hagmann leased Pal's to Don Drinkhouse and

Exterior of Pal's, with package room to the left, 1950s. *Author's collection.*

Ernest Gray and moved his office and operations to the Captain's Table. Drinkhouse and Gray promised a "new and different Pal's," switching to a gourmet dining experience. According to Drinkhouse, they were "introducing a special 'hospitality tray' (chilled black caviar and Roquefort cheese)" with a "lavish fruit bowl and imported swiss cheese" at a meal's end. "The name's the same but the plates are palatial, and palates will be treated royally," stated Drinkhouse. Prime ribs were the specialty, and the shrimp ernest and pompano amandine were highly recommended.

WFLM began live stereophonic programs (FM stereo radio broadcasts) from Pal's in October 1962. The Saturday night program featured music and interviews with restaurant patrons. In 1962, Pal's was awarded the White Horse Hospitality Award, which was presented annually to a restaurant with "exemplary cuisine, service and hospitality, carrying on today in the great traditions of the past." It was the first time that a local restaurant had won the award.

In early 1963, Drinkhouse and Gray redecorated the restaurant and reopened it as the Chalet East. It was closed in late July 1963. During the rest of the 1960s, the restaurant went through several iterations, including the Sunrise Fish House, Yankee Fisherman, Beefeater and the Beefeeder. It was slated to become Club Continental in 1969, but it never opened. It became Bachelors III in 1970. Today, a Bank of America branch occupies the site.

21

The Reef

In September 1943, Mr. and Mrs. Frederick Franke Sr. and their sons, Verne and Frederick Jr., arrived in Fort Lauderdale from Chicago, Illinois. There, they had operated Franke's Casino, a successful eatery for many years; it even operated as a speakeasy during Prohibition. They also owned and operated the Edgewater Apartments and the Seabreeze Restaurant (second floor of the Elbo Room). The family opened the Radio Club on November 15, 1945, at 2700 South Andrews Avenue. The building had formerly been occupied by the WFTL radio station but had been shut down during World War II, because the antennas were in the flight path of the naval air station (today the Fort Lauderdale-Hollywood International Airport). From 1948 to 1953, the Frankes leased the Radio Club out to other managers. In June 1954, Fred Franke Jr. announced plans for the remodeling and renaming of the Radio Club. It reopened on December 30, 1954, as Fred Franke's Reef. The redesign included the addition of coral rock walls, a stream flowing about the grounds and under bridges, a waterfall patio and two dining rooms—one featuring French cuisine and the other steak. The restaurant's main feature was its dual-tiered dance terraces, with an orchestra pit on a third terrace.

In early 1958, the Reef was sold to the Sam Zimmerman family, who owned a chain of dining and banquet facilities in New York and Connecticut, including the Chimney Corner Inn (Stamford, Connecticut) and Patricia Murphy's Candlelight (Manhasset, Long Island, New York). The restaurant was closed in September for a complete remodel. It

THE REEF RESTAURANT
INVITES
WEDDING RECEPTIONS
FOR THE BRIDE-TO-BE

R.S.V.P.   525-3435

MAKE YOUR RESERVATION NOW
Call JEAN HOPE, Banquet Coordinator

REEF
RESTAURANT

2700 S. ANDREWS AVE.   FORT LAUDERDALE

Advertisement promoting the Reef as a location for wedding receptions, 1965. *Courtesy of the Fort Lauderdale News.*

was transformed from a supper club to a family-type restaurant, with a revised menu that fit families' pocketbooks. The main dining room was renamed the Garden Room (formerly the Porpoise Room), which depicted Florida flowers. Fred Franke Jr. remained in the restaurant business by purchasing the Yardarm (Hillsboro Inlet) in 1959 and the Wharf (Lauderdale-By-The-Sea) in 1961; he opened the Bridge on East Oakland Park Boulevard in 1965 and acquired the Rampart Steak House (Lighthouse Point) in 1968.

For over twenty years, the Reef was one of the mainstays of the Fort Lauderdale catering and banquet business. According to Bob Freund of the *Fort Lauderdale News* (1964), "The Reef has enjoyed a steady reputation as one of the city's finest and most beautiful eating places." Robert Tolf, also of the *Fort Lauderdale News* (1976), concurred, "[It is] one of the best budget stops on the Gold Coast…putting out a menu [that is] consistently 50 to 70 percent less expensive than the competition far and near." Even after Sam Zimmerman's passing in November 1965, the family continued to operate the restaurant. In 1972, Sam's son, Larry "Zero," took over as the restaurant's general manager. Zero kept the restaurant running at peak efficiency and profit. "The Reef occupied an entire city block just north of the airport and could accommodate in its lounge, dining rooms and banquet rooms more than one thousand people a night," Zero Zimmerman recalled. "On Mother's Day and the entire holiday season, you couldn't get near the place. We had families and businesses make their reservations for the following year while they were checking out from their current dinners or parties."

The Reef featured American cuisine, including prime ribs of beef, roast turkey and some continental dishes, such as chicken kiev and veal parmiagiana; it also had a variety of seafood specialties. However, the restaurant's most popular dish was duck. Zero said, "The most memorable item on our menu was the complimentary popovers served with a tin of cottage cheese and strawberry rhubarb preserves." A 1978 *Fort Lauderdale News* article mentioned that, on a slow day, Chef Mike Marrero could turn out 3,600 popovers, but during "the season" he could bake at least 6,000.

The Reef was sold in 1981 and closed within a year. Today, a car lot for Abernathy's Auto Repair and Enterprise Rent-A-Car occupies the site.

22

Porky's Hide Away

After serving in the army air forces during World War II, Donald "Porky" Baines moved to Fort Lauderdale from Cleveland, Ohio. In 1949, he took over the operation of the Kabby Roll restaurant near the beach. After a couple of years, he decided to open a combination supper club and lounge called Porky's Restaurant at 309 South Federal Highway (just north of the Stranahan House). He sold that restaurant in 1954 and purchased a six-acre lot on the northwest corner of Northeast Thirty-Eighth Street and Federal Highway and opened Porky's Hide Away (3900 North Federal Highway) in 1955. His wife, Jean, was the cook, and she created a menu that featured steaks and barbecued meats.

Porky's featured various styles of house music that changed periodically. When it opened, Porky's showcased jazz musicians and featured many African American musicians and groups. Local musician and Dillard High School music teacher Julian "Cannonball" Adderley started his jazz group there. Later, in November 1959, Porky's started playing Dixieland music and, in January 1961, Calypso music. Porky's also featured headliners such as Guy Lombardo, Don Ho, Lawrence Welk, Conway Twitty and Flip Wilson. Additionally, local and out-of-state rock and roll bands played at Porky's. During spring break, college kids could drink all day at the bar for $1.50, and on Sunday afternoons, local teenagers were allowed in to hear the bands play. Baines also allegedly operated an underground fencing operation at Porky's, selling diamonds and fur coats. Although he was arrested multiple times, Baines always got off. Eventually, he was charged with tax evasion

Proprietor Donald "Porky" Baines at Porky's Hide Away. One of the earliest white venues to feature African American musicians and rock-and-roll bands. *Courtesy of History Fort Lauderdale, Gene Hyde Collection.*

on revenue from Porky's Hide Away and served time; this forced Porky's to close in 1967. However, Porky's lives on in local lore. It was the inspiration for the *Porky's* movie (1981), which was written and directed by former Fort Lauderdale resident Bob Clark. The abandoned building was later used for firefighter training and was burned down. Today, an LA Fitness Gym stands on the site.

23

The Round Table

The Round Table, which was opened in December 1961 at 3100 North Federal Highway, resembled a medieval castle or fortress with accompanying interior décor. The restaurant's owner was Gerson (George) Bacher, a former air force pilot who had been stationed at Boca Raton, Florida, during World War II. Prior to opening the Round Table, Bacher had operated the Pub in Coral Gables, Florida, since 1955.

The large, oak-beamed, red-carpeted eatery featured three giant open-hearth broilers, where steaks, chicken, chops and various shish kabobs were broiled right before patrons' eyes. A wide variety of seafoods, such as lobster and shrimp Newburg, were also served at the restaurant. The Round Table cut its own meats and didn't rely on pre-cut or pre-packaged meats. The restaurant's prices were skewed toward "the middle-class visitor and retired resident," catering to the diners who wanted a good steak and salad but couldn't afford the top prices. The Round Table's salad bar (which was reported to be the first in Fort Lauderdale) was said to be the most bountiful in town; it offered eighteen items and four dressings. The restaurant also served as the host for the weekly luncheon meeting (Fridays) of the Knights of the Round Table, a group of fifty local executives. In January 1963, the Round Table received the American Restaurant Hospitality Editorial Feature Award from *Hospitality* magazine for its outstanding service to the dining public, the community it served and the food service industry as a whole.

Exterior of the castle (Round Table), 1960s. *Author's collection.*

In late 1963, Bacher sold the restaurant to Southern Caterers Inc. (Gil Singer, Mark Kleines, Paul Schreiber and Cy Mandell). In 1967, Bacher regained control of the Round Table and started a $1,000 college scholarship that was sponsored by the restaurant. In 1969 and 1970, Bacher expanded the Round Table to Miami Beach and Hallandale, respectively. During the 1970s, Bacher and his partners built one of the most successful restaurant chains in South Florida. By 1979, they owned seven Round Table restaurants that grossed $15 million a year. Bacher introduced the "Odd Couple" (baked half chicken and sliced sirloin combo) in 1977, and when Jack Klugman tried it, he said, "At first, I was afraid it might taste like Tony Randall!" Bacher was also the inventor of the Econo-light (1974), an indicator light that alerted drivers when they were using too much fuel for a given situation; however, it did not catch on.

In May 1980, Bacher withdrew from managing the Round Tables, and in 1982, he split from his partners while retaining the Fort Lauderdale and Lauderdale Lakes locations. The Fort Lauderdale site went by the name of the Red Derby until 1984, when it was renamed Fulton Street Seafood (nautical theme); it was closed by 1986. George Bacher passed in 1999. Today, the site serves as a parking lot for the Coral Ridge Mall.

24

Sweden House Smorgasbord

Big John Albertson and John "Jack" Iding opened their first Sweden House in Elgin, Illinois, in December 1959; it was followed closely by a second location in Naperville, Illinois. In 1963, they partnered with Paul Glafenhein to open the first Florida (and third overall) location in Fort Lauderdale. Glafenhein was originally from Naperville and had purchased the Sand Castle Resort Motel in Fort Lauderdale in 1962.

The Sweden House was opened at 5550 North Federal Highway on November 22, 1963 (the day of the John F. Kennedy assassination), with Larry McGone as the manager (and partowner). Lunch at the restaurant originally cost $1.10, and dinner cost $2.10. A variety of foods (roast beef, chicken, shrimp, meatballs, vegetables, salads and desserts) were served at the restaurant. A May 1964 advertisement stated, "The most abundant variety of delicious foods ever set before your eyes! All at our famous low prices!" The restaurant had a full bakery with seating for nearly four hundred arranged in four dining rooms. The Sweden House's motto, as posted on their logo sign, was "all you care to eat." As a former customer remarked:

> During our yearly visits to Fort Lauderdale, in the 1960s and 1970s, we would go to the Sweden House. That was the only buffet restaurant we ever knew back then…and boy was it great food! And, yes, you could find "Swedish" meatballs. I also remember being very fond of their mashed potatoes and brown gravy…yummm! And all you can drink from the soda fountain machine (free refills were bizarre back in those years).

Three-part postcard showing the interior and exterior of the Sweden House, 1960s. *Author's collection.*

By 1971, Sweden House had ten locations (eventually there would be eighteen). At that time, the Fort Lauderdale location was the largest volume grosser in the chain ($1.2 million in 1970). Sunday and holiday dinners ran all day, from 11:00 a.m. to 9:00 p.m. The McGone children would run a one-dollar pool for the total number of customers. The record was set on Mother's Day 1968: 4,316. During the 1970s, the following radio commercial ran:

> *All you care to eat from our Smorgasbord*
> *Is here at a price you can easily afford.*
> *So, treat your children and please your spouse.*
> *Good taste makes the difference at Sweden House.*
> *All…you…care…to…eat!*

The food at Sweden House was so good and so plentiful that in its later years, it became all you can eat and all you can hide. A former assistant manager told the story of "Mr. and Mrs. Chicken Plucker." They were known to walk out with all kinds of fried chicken hidden on them, but the staff could never catch them. One minute, their plates were full of chicken, and the next minute, the plates were empty; and they were not eating it, as there were no bones.

Sweden House closed down in 1985, and Bea Morley's opened in its place in March 1986. Today, an Olive Garden stands on the site.

25
Chateau Madrid

The Chateau Madrid was located on the eighth (top) floor of the Kenann Building on the northwest corner of the intersection of Federal Highway and Oakland Park Boulevard (3101 North Federal Highway). The cylindrical landmark building was designed by Fort Lauderdale architect F. Louis Wolff for Ken and Ann Burnstine, and it was completed in 1964. It is said to have been inspired by *The Jetsons* cartoon and was always meant to be an eye-catcher. The exterior of the building featured a one-hundred-foot mural that was emblazoned with designs of tropical landscapes and sea life.

Unlike the Pier 66 Pier Top Dining Room, the Chateau Madrid did not rotate. Designed with a 220-seat dining area and a 60-seat cocktail lounge, the Chateau Madrid also had a parquet dance floor and bandstand. The restaurant also had exquisite panoramic views of Fort Lauderdale. Owned and operated by John and Dianne Bachan (previously a precision aircraft parts manufacturer), the restaurant was known as a high-end dining and entertainment venue, which featured a fabulous buffet, dining and dancing. Some of its entertainers over the years included Rosemary Clooney, Tony Martin, Benny Goodman, Patti Page, Johnny Mathis and Frankie Avalon. Louis Armstrong even played there for one week in 1966 and 1967, including on New Year's Eve; that dinner and show cost twenty-five dollars per person. Patricia Rucerito remembered "meeting both Louie Armstrong and Ella Fitzgerald after their performances here." In March 1967, The Men of *F Troop* tested out their act at the Chateau Madrid.

Left: Chateau Madrid postcard, with sketch of restaurant layout. *Courtesy of the Broward County Historical Archives, Broward County Library.*

Below: Advertisement for the "Men of F Troop" show at the Chateau Madrid, 1967. *Courtesy of Oldshowbiz.tumbler.com.*

Forrest Tucker, Ken Berry and Larry Storch were scheduled to do a live stage show in Reno, Nevada (April 10–May 3) and tried out their material in Fort Lauderdale to figure out what worked and what didn't. The show had them doing shtick as their *F Troop* characters before changing into tuxedos and doing individual nightclub acts.

The Bachans operated the restaurant as the Chateau Madrid until 1974, when they changed the name to the Rooftop. "People still talk about the fantastic free breakfast buffets and the all-you-can-eat Maine lobster dinners," Dianne Bachan's 2008 obituary stated. Lissa Calvert Dailey recalled, "That was one of the best date night places!" After the Bachans sold out, Chateau Madrid became the Rooftop restaurant (1974–87) before later becoming the Skytop Social and Fraternal Club. In January 2019, it was announced that Cornerstone Vacation Ownership's U.S. headquarters would occupy the eighth floor of the Kenann Building.

26
The Down Under

The Down Under was not named for its Australian cuisine and theme but rather for its location—it sat virtually under the Intracoastal Waterway Bridge, at 3000 East Oakland Park Boulevard. This "rather important waterfront tavern" was designed by architect Dan Duckham and featured a combination of designs that embraced features of Swiss chalets, western ranch houses, waterfront taverns and ski lodges, with touches of San Franciscan, New Orleans and Old New York designs. The creation of owners Leonce Picot and Al Kocab, the Down Under featured a turn-of-the-century atmosphere, which was enhanced by a blending of gaslights, oil lamps, Tiffany glass panels, antique furnishings and different woods, with a nautical touch. The restaurant's tables were refinished boat hatch covers, and utility poles served as support timbers. There were potted plants throughout, and fresh-cut flowers graced the tables. The 250-seat restaurant offered seating with views of the Intracoastal Waterway, as well as 150-feet of water frontage for docking boats. A seven-foot-tall wooden British guardsman kept a watchful eye over the patrons.

Kocab and Picot had previously coauthored and illustrated several restaurant guidebooks in the 1960s, including the *Great Restaurants of the United States and Their Recipes*. After touring many restaurants in major cities throughout the United States, they returned to Fort Lauderdale to start the Down Under. After opening on December 14, 1968, it offered a blend of American, French, Italian and English cuisine. German and Russian creations were later added to the menu. In addition to its eclectic mix of entrées, the Down Under featured

Al Kocab sketch of the Down Under. *Author's collection.*

an extraordinary wine list of over one hundred fine and prized wines ("The best" according to food critic Robert Tolf).

Over the years, the Down Under received numerous awards. In the September 1969 issue of *Esquire*, the restaurant received an outstanding mention. In the early 1970s, the Down Under was the only Florida restaurant to be chosen annually by *Esquire* to host a celebrity favorite dinner. It was presented with a *Mobil Tourist Guide* Award in 1972, and it won multiple Golden Spoon Awards from *Florida Trend* magazine. The Down Under was also awarded as a superior dining establishment by *Holiday* magazine for consecutive years in the 1970s. Its recipes were featured in the *Holiday Magazine Award Cookbook* (1974) and the Benson and Hedges 100s volume of *100 Recipes from 100 of the Greatest Restaurants* (1978).

A major part of the restaurant's success was Chef Christian Planchon, who worked there for twenty years. During the 1981 and 1985 inaugural celebrations of President Ronald Reagan, the Down Under was one of two Florida representatives at the "A Taste of America" celebration. It served lobster bisque in 1981 and marinated bay scallops in 1985. Picot and Kocab also opened La Vieille Maison (Boca Raton) in 1974 and Casa Vecchia in 1979. Al Kocab passed in 1994, and Picot sold the Down Under in late 1996. It was reopened as Pusser's Down Under in November 1996, before it became Pusser's Landing (1997–8) and, later, Pusser's West Indies (1999). The restaurant was officially closed around 2000, and the location is currently an empty lot.

27

Country Music Cabaret

Opened in December 1968, the Country Music Cabaret brought the sounds of Nashville to Fort Lauderdale. Located at 1432 North Federal Highway, this three-hundred-seat supper club was the first country western lounge east of Federal Highway. It offered an almost continuous show of country western artists for its patrons' listening and dancing pleasure. The Country Music Cabaret was owned by Bob Watson, who had been active in television, radio and nightclubs in Canada and the United States. This was his first foray as a club owner. The building had previously been home to Ken's Café Society and the Athena restaurants.

Aside from local country musicians, Watson's group, the Western Gentlemen, performed at the restaurant nightly. Some of the restaurant's local artists included Freddy King, Ricky King, Shirley Ray Sands and Tommy Overstreet and the Nashville Express. In August 1970, a Family Night (Tuesdays) was added to the restaurant's schedule, which offered free hot dogs for kids and screenings of old movies that starred the western stars of yesteryear. Wednesdays became talent nights, during which some of the aforementioned singers got their start.

Watson sold the County Music Cabaret to Moises Layun, an Argentinian businessman who had operated restaurants in Brazil and Detroit, in October 1970; the Western Gentleman continued to perform there. The lounge was expanded and remodeled in 1971. In the early to mid-1970s, Nashville stars began performing at the Country Music Cabaret. Hank Williams Jr. and Tanya Tucker were featured at the restaurant in 1973, and

Exterior of the Country Music Cabaret. *Courtesy of Scott Watson.*

Mel Tillis, Barbara Mandrell, Larry Gatlin and Ronnie Milsap also made appearances at the restaurant. In January 1977, a shift in entertainment policy toward more crossover and pop material caused the restaurant to shorten its name to just the Cabaret. In 1978, the restaurant's name and format were changed back.

After struggling through the Disco era, Layun sold the business in the summer of 1979 to Richard Tienken and Bob Wachs, the owners of New York's Comic Strip. In January 1980, it was reopened as the Comic Strip. Had Layun been able to hold on for one more year, he may have been able to cash in on the urban cowboy movement; however, a State Farm office stands on the site today.

28
Bachelors |||

"C ome on over and have a good time. I guarantee it." This is probably something that Bachelors III's part-owner Joe Namath might have said when the restaurant was opened on January 15, 1970. Opened in the former Pal's restaurant location, at 1745 East Sunrise Boulevard, Bachelors III was the second in a string of supper nightclubs that were owned by Bobby Van (Robert Vannuchi), Joe Namath (1968 AFL MVP and Super Bowl III MVP) and Ray Abruzzese (Namath's Alabama and New York Jet teammate). Featuring a menu of fine food (steaks and seafood), Bachelors III was the first club in Fort Lauderdale to present big-name entertainers year-round. Some of these performers included Bobby Vinton, James Brown, Jerry Lee Lewis, Ray Charles, Phyllis Diller, the Spinners, the Supremes, Freddie Prinz, Kool and the Gang and Brenda Lee.

Namath and Abruzzese sold their interests to Van after a couple of years. Van built Bachelors III from a small lounge in 1970 to South Florida's premiere big-name showcase by 1975 (it kept expanding its seating capacity). Bachelors III–West opened in Lauderdale Lakes in May 1975, but it was closed within a year. By mid-1976, Van was looking to sell Bachelors III, as booking top-flight talent was becoming too expensive for the venue. He sold it in January 1977 to a pair of Englishmen (John Connell and Vince Lee) who had operated supper clubs and casinos in London and Jamaica. The pair went bankrupt in April and skipped out of the country, leaving behind a large debt.

Advertisement promoting Della Reese (jazz and gospel singer, who later starred in *Touched by an Angel*), 1974. *Courtesy of the* Fort Lauderdale News.

During 1976 and 1977, Bobby Van opened Mr. Pip's, Mr. Laff's and the Candy Store. In early 1979, Van opened a new edition of Bachelors III at 2650 North Federal Highway. Designed by Dan Duckham, it was a three-part dining and entertainment complex (100-seat restaurant, 150-seat lounge and large entertainment room). It folded in July 1980 and later became the Silver Saddle Saloon (closed after a year). A Chick-Fil-A now sits on the site.

After the original Bachelors III closed in 1977, it became H.A. Winston & Co. in 1978 and, later, the Gathering (1980–4) and the Booby Trap (1986–8). Today, a Bank of America branch occupies the site.

29

Yesterday's

L ocated at 3001 East Oakland Park Boulevard, in the former Moonraker restaurant, Yesterday's was opened on October 29, 1975, in a two-story New England-style building. The Moonraker had been built and opened by Warren Foster in December 1966, with a nautical theme and décor. It was purchased by Cliff Rathmanner in late 1973, before he sold it to Arnold Grevior and Peter Goldhahn (later known as Peter Beck) in mid-1975. Grevior and Beck carried out a complete interior renovation to create an atmosphere that presented the best of the past. The lower level was devoted to dining, a second-floor terrace was screened in for outdoor dining, an open-air waterfront dining patio was added and the One-Up Lounge was located upstairs. "When Peter Beck bought it, the bottom level was called Moonraker, but the upstairs area was called Yesterday's," recalled waitress Terri Gardner. "He soon renamed the entire building Yesterday's and later named the upper lounge as The Plum Room."

Beck had previously operated the Fisherman restaurant, and he felt that Yesterday's would be the next logical step in building a cornerstone for his aspirations to present fine dining in an intimate atmosphere. The eight-hundred-seat waterfront (Intracoastal Waterway) restaurant was a favorite of visiting celebrities, and people would wait in line to dine, dance and drink with the likes of Frank Sinatra, John Travolta and Joe Namath. In October 1978, Jerry Lewis was dining in the Plum Room (he was in town scouting for the movie *Hardly Working*) while Iranian prince Raschid was at a nearby table.

On October 10, 1983, Burt Reynolds spent all day filming at Yesterday's for the movie *Stick* (the scene was cut from the film).

Yesterday's opened to great acclaim and reviews, and it soon became the place to go and be seen in Fort Lauderdale. The restaurant was the scene for wedding receptions, birthdays, anniversaries and prom nights. The menu featured fresh local and imported seafood and USDA prime beef. The chefs were constantly creating new specialties and revamped the menus regularly. In June 1978, baked hippopotamus, elk, fillet of rattlesnake and llama were added to the Plum Room's menu. Yesterday's also received numerous awards. In 1977, the restaurant was given an Epicurean Excellence Award from *Carte Blanche*. In November 1982, Yesterday's was granted the Award of Excellence from the Long Island Duck Farmers Cooperative for their Tahiti duck, and the Plum Room took the first place Top-of-the-Table award from *Restaurant Hospitality Magazine* in 1983.

Beginning in 1978, Beck began decorating the property for the winter holidays. Longtime manager Ginger Willis stated, "When we started getting compliments from passersby in cars and boats, in addition to our customers, Mr. Beck decided to keep the tradition going." At its peak, the entire display contained five trees and over five miles of lights. Yesterday's

Yesterday's, located along the Intracoastal Waterway, on the northwest corner of the Oakland Park Boulevard Bridge. *Courtesy of the State Archives of Florida, Florida Memory.*

won best restaurant multiple times in the Winterfest Boat Parade's shoreline decorating competition, and the restaurant received plaudits and attention from various media outlets around the world. Yesterday's was also the first (in South Florida) to utilize some restaurant innovations. In July 1979, they began offering Braille menus, and in September 1979, they introduced international language menus (French, German, Spanish). In 1980, Yesterday's began participating in the Creative Cuisine (heart healthy) program.

In the late 1990s, with national trends toward more casual dining, Yesterday's underwent a $1 million facelift in the hopes of luring in the masses with scaled-down prices. Renamed Moonraker's on the Water, the restaurant continued on until April 19, 2004, when it closed for good. The success of Yesterday's enabled Beck to create other popular local restaurants, including the Aruba Beach Café, H2O and the Casablanca Café. The building was demolished in 2009. Since 2016, the site has been home to the Symphony at the Waterway assisted living facility.

30

Historic Bryan Homes

The Tom and Reed Bryan Homes were built along the north bank of the New River in 1903, as parts of the Bryan Family Complex that was located along the west side of the FEC railway. Both men were integral parts of the early history of Fort Lauderdale. Tom was involved in farming and helped to establish a bank, the telephone service and the electric service in the town. Reed also took part in farming and built the first two dredges that cut the canal from Fort Lauderdale to Lake Okeechobee.

The Historic Tom and Reed Bryan Homes, which have served as various restaurants since 1983. *Author's Collection.*

In 1976, the City of Fort Lauderdale bought the property at 301 Southwest Third Avenue. Since 1983, when it was opened as the Historic Bryan Homes Restaurant by Anthony Gillette, the site has operated as a restaurant under a variety of names: the Chart House (1987–97), Reed's River House (1998) and the River House (1999–2009). The two homes were eventually merged into one facility, and for over twenty-five years, it was the place to go for an upscale meal, to celebrate weddings and retirements and to watch the boats go by. Increased building maintenance costs, declining business and a lack of on-site parking created operational issues.

When Anthony Gillette operated the restaurant, he spent two years researching to create his menu, which he called "the new Florida cuisine." It included recognizable Florida foods with a twist and historic dishes based on Native American and Moroccan foodstuffs. During the Chart House era, the restaurant had a nautical theme and cooked steak and seafood on an open grill. After being shuttered for eight years, James Campbell renovated the buildings and reopened the restaurant and banquet facility as the Old River House in 2017.

31
Ancient Mariner

The *Ancient Mariner* was Fort Lauderdale's first floating restaurant, and it was docked along the south bank of the New River, at Southeast Fifth Avenue, just west of Smoker Family Park. Originally built as a Prohibition Runner, the United States Coast Guard Cutter *Nemesis* (named after the Greek goddess of vengeance) served an honorable thirty-year stint as a World War II sub-chaser, escort convoy and rescue ship, and after the war, the boat patrolled the Florida coast. *Nemesis* was decommissioned in 1964, and it was auctioned off to Auto Marine Engineers.

Similar to the *Amphitrite* floating hotel, which was docked in Fort Lauderdale during the 1930s, the *Nemesis* became a converted naval vessel. In 1979, a group of investors bought the vessel and remodeled it to look like a three-deck African steamer. The boat was was renamed *Livingstone's Landing* and docked along the south bank of the New River to serve as a gourmet restaurant as part of an early downtown revitalization project. It closed two years later, citing management issues and poor business, despite receiving good reviews from restaurant critics.

After being sold and renamed the *Ancient Mariner*, the vessel sank on April 28, 1981, just two weeks before the grand reopening, due to small rust holes in its hull. This disaster resulted in $85,000 in damages, but it did not stop the restaurant from opening two months later. The *Ancient Mariner* was a success until bad luck struck again in 1986. The Broward County Public Health Unit shut down the restaurant on May 22, 1986, following a massive outbreak of hepatitis-A among 109 of its patrons (the largest food-

Looking south, across the New River, at the Ancient Mariner. *Courtesy of the Broward County Historical Archives, Broward County Library.*

borne hepatitis-A outbreak in Florida). The outbreak was traced back to a food prep worker. The restaurant could not survive the bad publicity and filed for bankruptcy.

Over the next five years, the restaurant changed owners and names multiple times. The vessel served as Chapman's River Raw Bar, Anchorage Seafood House, Dockside 501 and Cutters before closing down for good in October 1990. The boat was then purchased by the South Florida Divers Club of Hollywood for $6,000 in 1991, and the club donated it to Broward County's artificial reef program. In June of that year, the *Ancient Mariner* was sunk half a mile off Deerfield Beach. Today, the *Ancient Mariner* is thriving with sea life and is a popular dive site.

32
R Donuts

Drawing inspiration from a topless doughnut shop he had seen in Yuma, Arizona, on November 26, 1985 Andy Emery opened R Donuts, Fort Lauderdale's first topless doughnut shop. Housed in a former Burger King, the shop served up coffee, doughnuts and unfettered views of the waitresses. R Donuts was open from 6:00 a.m. to 8:00 p.m. daily and served ten different kinds of doughnuts. A cup of coffee and doughnuts cost one dollar each; sandwiches cost five dollars.

Unpopular with neighboring businesses (Tina's Spaghetti House was across the street), who feared that it would be a black mark on the area, the restaurant also faced picketers. However, R Donuts became popular over the years and carved a niche among European and Asian tourists, sailors, local businessmen and blue-collar workers. It received national and international features in newspapers and on radio and television programs. R Donuts opened to one customer, a cab driver named Mark Johnson, and thirteen news reporters and camera crews. Johnson remarked, "I think it's a great idea for 6:00 a.m. in the morning. Where else can you get a breakfast like this at this time of day? It's the best doughnut I've ever had." Over five hundred customers stopped by during the first day. Early on, R Donuts was attracting as many as one thousand customers a day. In its later years, the shop served, on average, between sixty and eighty patrons per day. Once, when asked what made his business so successful, Emery replied, "I'd say pretty girls and the world's best coffee."

First customer, Mark Johnson, checking out the coffee and doughnuts—and waitress Charlotte—at the grand opening of R Donuts on November 26, 1985. *Courtesy of the Sun-Sentinel.*

In February 1986, the *Fort Lauderdale News* sent over a review crew of reporters and editors who determined unanimously that the "décor" was slightly distracting and that the doughnuts were average. R Donuts also sponsored a women's team (no employees) in the Sunrise Softball League during 1986. The players' only concern was the store logo (similar to the Hooters logo) on the team shirts.

R Donuts closed on July 30, 1990, following the death of Emery. He passed away on April 9, after he and his waitresses had delivered coffee and doughnuts to the sailors on the yachts in the Whitbread 'Round the World Race at Pier 66 in the pouring rain. Today, the Lauderdale Mini dealership is located on the site.

Epilogue

In a little over 125 years, Fort Lauderdale has grown from a sleepy farming community to a land boom town, then a small Depression-era resort city to a World War II training center with postwar suburban growth and finally into today's world-class tourist resort town. Gastronomical delights are alive and well in Fort Lauderdale. The city has a long tradition of providing a variety of restaurants and food choices; some have standard fare while others have local flare.

These restaurants have played host to locals and visitors alike, including winter visitors (our snowbirds) since the earliest days. It was and is not unusual to see nationally known singers and entertainers performing and dining in Fort Lauderdale. Movie stars, royals, sports stars and celebrities of all types have taken the opportunity to sit and eat at Fort Lauderdale's dining establishments. Some have even had ownership stakes. Community groups and civic organizations have held weekly meetings, awards banquets and fundraising events at many of these local restaurants. Wedding receptions, anniversaries, holiday dinners, prom dates, boys' and girls' nights and first dates have been celebrated in these now-closed—but not forgotten—eateries. Many of these buildings and locations have gone through multiple iterations as many different restaurants. Many of these sites are still currently serving as eateries.

Hopefully, this perusal of Fort Lauderdale's dining past will spark your interest in the history of this great town; perhaps it will remind you of memories of its restaurants of old and entice you to eat at one of the current great dining establishments in Fort Lauderdale.

Vintage Recipes

MAGUIRE'S HILL 16
Potato Soup

2 tablespoons unsalted butter
6 medium all-purpose potatoes (about 3½ pounds),
peeled and cut into ¼-inch dice
2 medium onions, peeled and coarsely chopped
6 cups good chicken stock
salt and fresh-ground white pepper, to taste
chopped parsley, for garnish

Melt the butter in a large skillet over medium heat. Stir in the potatoes and onions, cover and gently cook the vegetables, stirring occasionally, for about twelve minutes or until soft but not browned. Add the stock and season with salt and white pepper.

Place about 1½ cups of the cooked vegetables with a little of their liquid in a blender or food processor fitted with a metal blade and puree. Stir this back into the remaining potatoes that were left diced for texture. Serve the soup in warmed bowls and sprinkle with parsley. Recipe makes six (1½-cup) servings.

❖ ❖ ❖

MANGO'S
Snow Crab Bisque

6 ounces (1 ½ sticks) unsalted butter
8 ounces button mushrooms, sliced
⅓ cup fine-diced onions
⅓ cup fine-diced green bell peppers
⅓ cup chopped scallions, white and one inch of green
⅓ cup sherry wine
½ teaspoon Tabasco sauce
¼ teaspoon cayenne pepper (or to taste)
¼ teaspoon ground white pepper (or to taste)
½ teaspoon salt (or to taste)
¾ cup all-purpose flour
3 cups milk
1 ½ cups half-and-half
1 pound cooked snow crab meat
¼ cup chopped fresh parsley

Using a large saucepan over medium heat, melt the butter. Add the mushrooms, onions, green peppers and scallions. Cover and cook the vegetables, stirring frequently, until they start to release their juices (about fifteen minutes).

Add the sherry, Tabasco, cayenne, white pepper and salt. Increase heat to high and boil for one minute.

Reduce heat to medium-low and gradually add flour. Cook, stirring constantly, for three to four minutes. Slowly add milk and half-and-half. Cook, stirring occasionally, until simmering (about fifteen minutes); be careful not to scorch.

Add the crab meat and parsley and cook, stirring occasionally, for three to four minutes. Adjust seasoning, if necessary. Makes twelve servings.

SHIRTTAIL CHARLIE'S
Conch Chowder

¾ pound cleaned and tenderized conch
3 ribs celery, chopped
1 onion, diced
¾ cup frozen green peas
¾ cup frozen corn kernels
1 green bell pepper, seeded and diced
1½ teaspoons lemon juice
1½ teaspoons dry sherry
¾ teaspoon fresh ground black pepper
¾ teaspoon dried basil
¾ teaspoon dried oregano
¾ teaspoon dried thyme
1 bay leaf
¼ teaspoon Old Bay Seasoning
¼ teaspoon dried red pepper flakes
¼ teaspoon chicken base
14½-ounce can fresh-diced new potatoes, drained
28-ounce can diced tomatoes in tomato juice
2 tablespoons tomato paste
1 cup water

Using a food processor fitted with metal blade, use about six on/off pulses to chop conch. Leave some texture; do not turn into a paste. In a nonreactive large pot or Dutch oven, combine all ingredients. Bring to a boil, reduce heat and simmer for one hour. Makes eight cups, or two quarts.

LE DÔME
Veal Oscar

bearnaise sauce
18 fresh, slender asparagus spears
6 veal cutlets (about 1 pound)
1 egg, slightly beaten
1 tablespoon water
¾ cup dry breadcrumbs
½ teaspoon salt
½ teaspoon fresh-ground black pepper
½ cup all-purpose flour
2 tablespoons butter or margarine
2 tablespoons vegetable oil
12 ounces fresh lump crabmeat (well drained, if using canned)
3 tablespoons chopped parsley, for garnish
4 pompano fillets, 8 ounces each
1 carrot, cut julienne style
2 celery sticks, cut julienne style

Prepare bearnaise sauce and keep warm.

Cut tough bottoms off of the asparagus spears (spears should be three to four inches long); set aside.

With a meat mallet, pound veal cutlets until they are ¼ inch thick. Cut into serving pieces. In a wide, shallow bowl, mix breadcrumbs, salt and pepper. Place flour in a second shallow bowl.

Dredge veal with flour, then dip into egg mixture and coat with breadcrumb mixture. Heat 1 tablespoon of the butter or margarine and 1 tablespoon of the oil in a ten-inch skillet over medium heat until hot. Cook half of the cutlets, turning once, until golden brown and cooked through (two to three minutes per side).

Remove veal to paper-towel-lined plate to drain and keep warm. Repeat with remaining butter or margarine, oil and veal.

In boiling water, blanch asparagus until tender-crisp; drain well. Place veal on warm serving plate, top with lump crabmeat and three blanched asparagus spears. Ladle on warm bearnaise sauce and sprinkle with parsley. Serve immediately. Makes six servings.

BRAVO RISTORANTE
Ziti Chicken (Con Pollo) Primavera

Spicy Cake
¾ cup olive oil
1 tablespoon chopped fresh rosemary
1 tablespoon chopped fresh oregano
1 tablespoon chopped fresh parsley
1 tablespoon chopped fresh basil
5 large garlic cloves, sliced
1 pound chicken tenderloins, trimmed

In a large bowl, combine all the ingredients except the chicken. Submerge the chicken in the mixture and stir to make sure the chicken is well coated. Refrigerate for at least two hours. To cook, remove chicken from marinade, letting as much as possible drain off. Discard the marinade.

Heat a grill to medium heat. Grill chicken until cooked through (about three minutes per side, depending on thickness). Alternately, using a large nonstick sauté pan over medium heat, sauté the chicken until just cooked through (about three minutes per side). No extra oil is needed for sautéing due to the oil in marinade. Transfer to a plate and tent with foil to keep warm until needed.

Francese Sauce
4 tablespoons butter
¼ cup white wine
6 tablespoons chicken broth
¼ cup fresh lemon juice

In a small saucepan over medium heat, combine all of the ingredients and slowly bring to a boil while stirring. Reduce heat and simmer for about five minutes; remove from the heat and set aside at room temperature. If made far in advance, the butter will solidify on top; in that case, reheat slowly over low heat before adding to the pasta.

Pasta and Vegetables
½ cup olive oil
5 large garlic cloves, peeled and sliced

1 cup chicken broth
1 cup white wine
1 tablespoon chopped fresh rosemary
1 tablespoon chopped fresh oregano
1 tablespoon chopped fresh parsley
1 tablespoon chopped fresh basil
pinch dry oregano
½ teaspoon onion powder
1 cup broccoli florets
½ cup julienned carrots
½ cup button mushrooms
½ cup chopped onions
4 canned artichoke hearts, drained and quartered
½ cup red bell peppers
½ cup yellow bell peppers
½ cup green bell peppers
8 ounces ziti, cooked according to package directions
kosher salt and fresh-ground black pepper, to taste
½ cup fresh-grated parmesan cheese, for garnish

In a large sauté pan, over medium heat, heat the oil. Sauté the garlic until just softened (about two minutes). Add the chicken broth, fresh herbs, dry oregano and onion powder. Bring to a boil over medium-high heat. Reduce heat and simmer, stirring occasionally, for seven to eight minutes or until the liquid is reduced by about a third.

Add the vegetables, return to simmer and cook until just barely soft (about three minutes). Add chicken to vegetable mixture and let cook until warmed through. Add the sauce and cooked ziti; toss well to combine. Season with salt and pepper, to taste.

To serve, divide the pasta among four large, warm bowls and top each serving with about ⅛ cup parmesan cheese. Makes four servings.

LEFT BANK
Baked Pompano with Avocado in Saffron Consommé

4 pompano fillets, 8 ounces each
1 carrot, cut julienne style
2 celery sticks, cut julienne style
1 tomato, diced
1 shallot, finely chopped
½ cup dry white vermouth
½ cup fish stock
¼ teaspoon saffron
1 tablespoon chopped fresh parsley
juice of 1 lemon
salt and pepper, to taste
2 medium-size avocados
2 tablespoons sweet butter

Preheat oven to 350 degrees Fahrenheit. Place fillets side by side in a shallow baking dish. Add carrot, celery, tomato, shallot, vermouth, fish stock, saffron, parsley and lemon juice. Add salt and pepper to taste. Cover with a buttered sheet of aluminum foil and bake for ten minutes.

In the meantime, using a melon baller, scoop out two dozen avocado balls about a half inch in diameter. In a small skillet, heat two pounds of butter, add the avocado balls and, stirring gently, sauté for five minutes on a low to medium heat setting.

Remove the fish from the oven and place fillets on a warm serving platter. Transfer consommé to the skillet with the avocado balls. Reduce for five minutes, pour over the fillets and serve immediately. Makes four servings.

❖ ❖ ❖

MAI-KAI
Macadamia Nut–Encrusted Mahi-Mahi with Tropical Fruit Sauce

Tropical Fruit Sauce
3 ounces papaya, peeled and diced (about 1 cup cut into ½-inch dice)
3 ounces mango, peeled and diced (about ¾ cup cut into ½-inch dice)
3 ounces pineapple, peeled and diced (about ¾ cup cut into ½-inch dice)
1 large navel orange, peeled and sectioned
1 ½ tablespoons Grand Marnier or other orange-flavored liqueur
½ cup apple cider vinegar
1 cup and 2 tablespoons fresh orange juice, divided
½ cup firm-packed dark brown sugar
1 tablespoon cornstarch

Nut-Encrusted Mahi-Mahi
1 cup macadamia nuts, fine-chopped and toasted*
¼ teaspoon minced garlic
½ teaspoon dried basil
1 teaspoon minced cilantro
½ cup all-purpose flour
2 large eggs, lightly beaten
4 mahi-mahi fillets (6 to 7 ounces each)
salt and fresh-ground black pepper, to taste
2 tablespoons unsalted butter
2 tablespoons vegetable oil

To make the sauce, in a large nonreactive mixing bowl, combine the papaya, mango, pineapple and orange pieces. Drizzle the Grand Marnier over the fruit and toss gently. Let stand at room temperature for about one hour.

Meanwhile, in a heavy nonreactive saucepan, mix together the vinegar, one cup of orange juice and sugar. Bring to a boil over medium-high heat while stirring. Reduce heat and simmer for about six minutes, stirring frequently, until reduced by a quarter. Add the marinated fruits with juices. Stir the cornstarch into the remaining two tablespoons of orange juice and gradually stir into the hot fruit mixture until thickened. It should be the consistency of very heavy cream. Since the juices in the fruits vary, you may need a bit more or a bit less of the cornstarch mixture.

The sauce can be made several hours or even a full day ahead of time and refrigerated. Just before serving, heat slowly, stirring occasionally. By chance, if you think the sauce is too thick, just add a bit more orange juice. Serve hot.

To make the fish, in a food processor that is fitted with a metal blade or a good blender, process the nuts, garlic, basil and cilantro briefly until well mixed and finely ground. Transfer to one of the 7 × 4½ × 1 inch gratin dishes (or something similar in size).

Place the flour in a second gratin or similar dish and add the eggs in the third.

Remove any skin and bones from the fillets. Sprinkle each side with salt and pepper. Turn the fillets in the flour, then the eggs and finally in the macadamia mix, pressing gently to help the mixture adhere.

In a large, heavy skillet—preferably nonstick—melt the butter with the oil over medium-high heat. Sauté the fillets for about three minutes on each side, or until well-browned and just cooked through. Divide the fillets among four warmed serving dishes and spoon the tropical fruit sauce on top. Makes four servings.

To roast the macadamia nuts, preheat the oven to 350 degrees Fahrenheit; spread a heaping cup of nuts on a baking sheet with sides. Bake for six to eight minutes, or until fragrant and just beginning to take on color. Cool completely before chopping.

MEJICO GRANDE
Enchiladas de Jocoqui

Enchiladas Sauce
½ clove garlic
1 teaspoon oregano
1 15-ounce can of tomato sauce
2 tablespoons tomato paste
2 tablespoons oil
1 teaspoon salt
1 teaspoon chili powder
1 teaspoon cumin

Simple Taco Mix
1 tablespoon salt
1 teaspoon pepper
¼ teaspoon cayenne pepper
1 tablespoon chili powder
1 teaspoon oregano

Main Recipe
1 pound chopped beef round
6 tortillas
1 minced onion
½ pound grated cheddar cheese
1 pint sour cream
shredded lettuce

To make the sauce, in a blender, grind the garlic, oregano and tomato sauce. Add to hot oil and simmer gently for fifteen minutes. Add salt, cumin and chili powder. Stir and let stand.

To make the taco mix, mix together salt, pepper, cayenne pepper, chili powder and oregano.

Pan fry beef and render the fat. Add taco mix to meat. Dip tortillas in hot oil and roll beef into tortillas. Place in a baking dish. Cover with enchilada sauce. Top with cheese and bake at 350 degrees Fahrenheit for twenty minutes. Top with desired amount of sour cream and garnish with shredded lettuce.

LE CAFÉ DE PARIS
Chicken Française with Spinach Noodles

4 whole chicken breasts, boned, skinned and split in half
flour for dredging chicken
about 2 to 3 tablespoons vegetable oil
2 tablespoons butter

Lemon Wine Sauce
½ pound butter
juice from 2 lemons
¼ cup white wine

Egg Wash
2 to 3 eggs, beaten
½ cup milk
1 teaspoon salt
¼ teaspoon white pepper

Spinach Noodles
1 pound spinach noodles
½ cup olive oil
4 cloves garlic, crushed and chopped
salt and pepper, to taste

Skin and bone chicken breasts. With a wooden mallet, pound chicken breasts between two sheets of waxed paper or parchment baking paper until flat. Wrap chicken breasts individually and place in refrigerator.

To prepare the lemon wine sauce, melt the butter in a saucepan. Add lemon juice and bring to a boil. Add white wine and reduce heat. Keep warm over very low heat.

Prepare egg wash by combining beaten eggs with milk, salt and pepper. Dredge chicken breasts in flour, then dip in egg wash.

In a large skillet, pour in enough oil to cover the bottom of the pan and add two tablespoons of butter. When the oil and butter mixture is hot, add chicken breasts and sauté on each side until they are light golden brown (no more than a few minutes or they will overcook and become tough). Place chicken on large, flat baking dish. Pour lemon wine sauce over chicken and place in the oven (150 to 200 degrees Fahrenheit) to keep warm.

In large saucepan, boil water (about six cups). Add spinach noodles and bring to a boil again. Cover and cook over low heat for ten to fifteen minutes until noodles are tender. Drain and rinse noodles under hot water. Pour olive oil in the same saucepan and heat. Add chopped garlic. When garlic sizzles, return noodles to pot and mix with the garlic and olive oil mixture until noodles are thoroughly coated. Serve noodles immediately with chicken breasts. Serves eight.

YESTERDAY'S
Scallops with Sweet Potato Crust

1 large piece of boniato (Caribbean white sweet potato), about 1 pound
8 large, fresh sea scallops
1 ½ tablespoons cornstarch
salt and fresh-ground white pepper, to taste
1 large egg white, lightly beaten
oil for deep frying
1 tablespoon Chinese rice wine vinegar or lemon juice
¼ cup light olive oil
2 cups bite-sized pieces mixed greens

Peel the boniato and grate it on the large holes of a hand grater (a box-type grater works well for this). You should have about 1 ½ cups grated boniato. Dry well with paper towels and separate the strands into a bowl.

Remove any muscles from the sides of the scallops. Rinse under cool water and pat dry with paper towels.

Place the cornstarch in a small bowl and season with salt and pepper. Place the egg white in another small bowl.

Place enough oil in a large, heavy saucepan to measure 1 ½ inches deep; heat over a medium-high heat until it reaches 365 degrees Fahrenheit on a candy thermometer.

While the oil is heating, whisk together the vinegar and oil in a nonreactive container to form a vinaigrette.

Dust the scallops with the cornstarch, dip in the egg white and press the grated boniato onto all sides of the coated scallops. Place on paper towels while dipping and pressing the remaining scallops.

As soon as the oil reaches 365 degrees Fahrenheit, lower the scallops into the pan with a slotted spoon. Keep an eye on the heat and adjust it to maintain an even temperature. Fry the scallops, turning if necessary, for about three minutes or until they are nicely browned on all sides and just cooked through. Drain well on paper towels.

Divide the greens between two serving dishes. Arrange the scallops on the greens and, after whisking again, drain the vinaigrette over the dish. Makes two servings.

❖ ❖ ❖

THE CAVES
Key Lime Baked Alaska

Graham Cracker Crust
1 cup graham cracker crumbs (about sixteen squares)
¼ cup sugar
⅓ cup melted butter
½ cup chopped walnuts

Key Lime and Ice Cream Fillings
2 quarts good-quality vanilla ice cream
1 14-ounce can of sweetened condensed milk
2 tablespoons water
3 large egg yolks
½ cup Key lime juice

Italian Meringue
1 ½ cups sugar
½ cup water
4 large eggs whites
pinch cream of tartar

To make the crust, lightly oil the side of an eight-inch springform pan. Combine all of the ingredients well; press into the bottom and about a half inch up the side of the prepared pan. Place in the freezer.

To make the fillings, soften one quart of ice cream in a large mixing bowl until it can easily be spread. Spoon the ice cream onto the cold crust and smooth into an even layer. Place in the freezer until solid.

While that layer is freezing, prepare the Key lime layer. Place the half cup of milk, water and egg yolks in a heavy nonreactive saucepan over low heat (or in the top of a double boiler over barely simmering water). Whisk the ingredients together and continue whisking constantly until the mixture thickens and the temperature reaches 160 degrees Fahrenheit. This will take ten to fifteen minutes; you want to do it slowly to prevent the yolks from curdling.

Remove the top of the pan from the heat and place in a bowl of cold water. Keep whisking until the mixture comes to room temperature. Stir in the remaining milk and the Key lime juice. Refrigerate for about one hour or until thickened and chilled. Spread evenly on top of the ice cream layer in the springform pan. Return to the freezer and allow the lime layer to harden.

When the lime layer is firm, soften the remaining quart of ice cream to spreading consistency and spread evenly over the lime layer. Your springform pan will be full to the top. Return to the freezer, and when it is completely frozen, cover with aluminum foil.

To make meringue, stir together the sugar and water in a heavy saucepan. Bring to a boil slowly over medium-high heat, stirring to melt the sugar. As soon as the mixture is clear and begins to boil, stop stirring. Let the mixture boil until it reaches a temperature of 240 degrees Fahrenheit on a candy thermometer. This is when the meringue is in the soft ball stage or the thread stage (the mixture will spin a thread about six inches long when lifted with a spoon).

While the syrup is cooking, preheat the oven broiler. In a large, clean bowl, beat the egg whites on medium speed until foamy. Add the cream of tartar and continue beating on high until stiff peaks form. When the syrup is ready, continue beating the egg whites on medium speed, dribbling the hot syrup into them until it is all used. Continue beating on medium speed until the mixture reaches room temperature and is very stiff. You should be able to draw a spatula through it and have it remain erect on either side of the spatula's path.

Run a knife around the inside of the springform pan and release the side. Place the dessert on a heat-proof serving platter or board. Quickly cover the top and side with the meringue, making sure it is at least ½ to 1 inch thick all around and that it covers the sides completely, down to the serving platter or board. Place in the oven about three inches from the heat source. Broil for ten to fifteen seconds or until nicely browned. Serve at once or place it back in the freezer for up to three days. Makes twelve servings.

HISTORIC BRYAN HOMES RESTAURANT
Bartlett Pears Mary Ashe

Pears
3 cups water
3 cups granulated sugar
⅓ cup or 3 ounces pear liqueur
4 Bartlett pears, peeled

Pastry Cream
1 cup milk
3 tablespoons all-purpose flour
¼ cup confectioners' sugar
3 egg yolks
1 teaspoon vanilla extract

White Chocolate Sauce
2 cups milk
8 ounces high-quality white chocolate, coarsely chopped
2 tablespoons flour
6 egg yolks
1 teaspoon vanilla extract

Egg Wash
3 eggs
¼ cup heavy cream
¼ cup milk

Coatings
1½ cups flour
1½ cups fresh white breadcrumbs
3 to 4 cups vegetable oil

To prepare the pears, mix together the water, sugar and pear liqueur in a large saucepan over medium high heat. Poach the pears in the liquid for about twelve minutes or until tender. Using a slotted spoon, remove the pears from the saucepan and cool at room temperature. Refrigerate overnight.

Make the pastry cream in a double boiler over hot—not simmering—water. Combine the milk, flour and confectioners' sugar. Whisk by hand until the mixture thickens and cook for two minutes.

Add the egg yolks and continue to whisk. Do not allow the mixture to boil. Transfer the pastry cream to a medium bowl, add the vanilla and whisk in the butter. Refrigerate, covered, overnight.

To make the white chocolate sauce, combine 1¾ cups milk and the white chocolate in a double boiler over hot—not simmering—water, and heat until the chocolate is just melted.

Place the flour in a small bowl. Slowly add the remaining milk and whisk until a smooth paste forms. Add this mixture to the melted white chocolate mixture and whisk over low heat for about two more minutes until the sauce thickens. Add the egg yolks and whisk for about one more minute. Remove from heat and add the vanilla.

Before frying the pears, prepare the egg wash by combining the eggs, heavy cream and milk. Cut off one inch of the bottom of each pear and reserve. Core the pears and spoon the chilled pastry cream inside. Replace the bottom of each pear, using wooden toothpicks to hold them in place.

To bread the pears, coat them first with flour, then dip them in the egg wash and roll them in the breadcrumbs. Heat the oil to 370 degrees Fahrenheit in a heavy saucepan. Deep fry the pears for about two minutes or just until they are golden. Remove the fried pears from the oil with a slotted spoon and place them in paper towels to drain. Carefully remove the toothpicks before serving.

To assemble the pears, spoon a pool of warm white chocolate sauce unto each dessert plate. Place a warm fried pear in the center of the sauce and serve. Makes four servings.

BURT AND JACK'S
Sticky Toffee Pudding

Spicy Cake
6 ounces pitted dates
1 ¼ cups water
1 teaspoon baking soda
1 stick (½ cup) unsalted butter, at room temperature
1 cup firm-packed dark brown sugar
2 large eggs
2 teaspoons dark molasses
1 ¼ cups all-purpose flour
2 teaspoons baking powder

Dark Sauce
1 stick (½ cup) unsalted butter
1 cup firm-packed dark brown sugar
1 cup heavy cream
1 tablespoon dark rum (we like Meyer's Original Dark)
2 teaspoons dark molasses

To make the cake, cover the dates with the water and bring to a boil in a medium saucepan over medium-high heat. Reduce the heat and simmer the dates for about twenty-five minutes or until the liquid is completely gone and the dates are like mush.

Use a wooden spoon to stir them occasionally and to mash them as they soften. Stir in the baking soda and let the mixture cool to room temperature.

Preheat the oven to 325 degrees Fahrenheit. Spray a twelve-cup Bundt pan well with no-stick cooking spray.

Using an electric mixer on medium, cream the butter and sugar until it is light and fluffy, then add the eggs, one at a time, beating well after each addition. Stir in the molasses, flour and baking powder. Lastly, stir in the cooked dates, making sure they are well-incorporated.

Spoon the mixture into the prepared Bundt pan. Bake in the center of the oven for twenty-five to thirty minutes or until it is firm to the touch and beginning to pull away from the sides of the pan. Remove cake to a wire rack and let cool in the pan for five minutes. Invert onto the wire rack and let cool to room temperature.

To make the sauce, melt the butter in a medium heavy saucepan over medium heat. Add the sugar and stir until dissolved. Stir in the cream, rum and molasses and bring to a boil. Remove from the heat. The sauce is best served warm over the room-temperature cake.

To serve, cut the cake into eight pieces. Cut each piece in half vertically. Place two halves on each serving plate—cut side down—with the inside edges touching. Spoon a heaping fourth of a cup of the warm sauce over each serving. Makes eight servings.

WHO SONG'S AND LARRY
Corn Cakes

1 ½ cups corn kernels, either defrosted frozen or drained from a can
¼ cup yellow cornmeal
¼ cup sugar
¼ teaspoon salt
½ teaspoon baking powder
1 stick (½ cup) butter, at room temperature
⅓ cup masa harina
¼ cup room-temperature water
3 tablespoons heavy cream

Preheat oven to 375 degrees Fahrenheit. Butter an eight-inch square baking dish. Set aside.

In a blender or food processor fitted with a metal blade, use on/off pulses to coarsely chop corn. You don't want a purée but a mixture with some whole kernels in it; set it aside.

In a large bowl, whisk together cornmeal, sugar, salt and baking powder. Transfer to a piece of wax paper. In the same bowl, using an electric mixer on medium speed, cream butter and masa harina until smooth. Stir in chopped corn, water and heavy cream. Add dry ingredients and stir thoroughly.

Transfer to prepared baking dish, smoothing top. Place dish in a larger baking dish. Place on middle shelf of oven, then fill a larger dish with enough hot water to come halfway up the dish with batter in it. Bake for fifty to sixty minutes or until cooked through. The center will remain moist but firm. Remove the small dish from the water bath and let it sit for fifteen minutes on a wire rack. To serve, scoop out portions with an ice cream scoop or with a large serving spoon. Makes sixteen servings.

THE DOWN UNDER
Quiche Michele

1 cup sliced fresh mushrooms
½ cup diced ham
2 tablespoons butter
2 beaten eggs
1 cup whipping cream
½ cup (2 ounces) shredded cheddar cheese
¼ teaspoon ground nutmeg
½ teaspoon salt
dash pepper
1 9-inch baked quiche or pie shell

In a saucepan, cook mushrooms and ham in butter until mushrooms are tender (about five minutes). Set aside. In a mixing bowl, combine eggs, cream, cheese, nutmeg, salt and pepper.

Place the ham and mushroom mixture in the bottom of a baked shell; pour egg mixture on top. Bake in an oven at 350 degrees Fahrenheit for twenty-five minutes. Let stand for ten minutes before serving. Makes one 9-inch quiche.

Bibliography

Articles

Bacher, George. "Restaurant Owner Faces Facts." *Fort Lauderdale News*, September 5, 1963.

Barszewski, Larry. "Historic River House Property to get New Life in Lauderdale." *Sun-Sentinel*, July 13, 2015.

Bender, Virginia. "Shirttail Charlie's For That 'Different' Business Lunch." *Fort Lauderdale News and Sun-Sentinel*, December 23, 1984.

Bien, William. "Broward Business Scene." *Fort Lauderdale Daily News*, July 31, 1957.

Bondurant, Bill. "Bachelor's III Invade Ft. Lauderdale." *Fort Lauderdale News*, December 31, 1969.

Brazer, Joan. "Belly Dancer a Bonus at Maharaja." *Fort Lauderdale News*, June 13, 1974.

———. "Eduardo's Trade Good." *Fort Lauderdale News*, August 16, 1974.

Brown, Pat. "Nashville Sound Shakes the Rafters in New Cabaret." *Fort Lauderdale News*, December 2, 1968.

———. "New Kim's Cabin Open." *Fort Lauderdale News*, April 14, 1967.

———. "New Owner Remodels Sierra Inn, Upgrades Menu." *Fort Lauderdale News and Sun-Sentinel*, June 30, 1968.

———. "Rain Dancer Readies Pit, Tavern Opening." *Fort Lauderdale News and Sun-Sentinel*, December 19, 1971.

————. "Sea Horse Restaurant Getting a Complete New Look." *Fort Lauderdale News and Sun-Sentinel*, October 4, 1964.

Carson, Paul. "Le Dôme's Menu Spiced by Success." *Fort Lauderdale News*, February 15, 1977.

Casey, Dave. "Beach Landmark, Student Prince, Closing Its Doors." *Fort Lauderdale News and Sun-Sentinel*, April 27, 1980.

Connelly, Michael. "Shop's Scenery, Not Doughnuts, Real Eye-Opener for Customers." *Fort Lauderdale News/Sun-Sentinel*, November 28, 1985.

Copeland, Mary. "'Pot Roast Table' Etched in History." *Miami Herald*, February 3, 1974.

Courier-Journal (Louisville, KY). "Chain-Restaurant Operator Jerome M. Lederer Dies." February 18, 1963.

deGroot, John. "Eating It All." *Fort Lauderdale News*, July 22, 1984.

De la Cruz, Ralph. "The Scoop on Ice Cream Cones." *Sun-Sentinel*, June 3, 2003.

d'Oliveira, Stephen. "Final Mooring for 'Ancient Mariner,' It's 'Water, Water Everywhere.'" *Sun-Sentinel*, June 10, 1991.

Eiland, Darrell. "1.5 Million Pounds of Roast Beef Later, Landmark to Close." *Miami Herald*, August 22, 1986.

Elich, Patricia. "'Hot Rodders' Roast Beef Stand to Close." *Sun-Sentinel*, August 16, 1986.

Fort Lauderdale Daily News. "Chinese Cafes Cater to Tastes of City Diner." August 14, 1946.

————. "New Restaurant Opens Today." February 11, 1956.

————. "Restaurateur Dies Suddenly." January 21, 1952.

Fort Lauderdale News. "'Beachcombing' Wilsons Swapped Salt for Sand." September 25, 1959.

————. "Chef's Choice…From the Reef." November 1, 1978.

————. "Gus Ducas, Original Owner of Tina's Spaghetti House." January 18, 1986.

————. "La Scala Due New Name, Owner." October 9, 1970.

————. "Restaurant to Open." February 21, 1959.

————. "Student Prince Gives Beach Tyrolean Touch." May 6, 1960.

————. "There's a Little Bit of Everything in New Intracoastal Dining Spot." December 16, 1968.

Fort Lauderdale News and *Sun-Sentinel*. "Fire Sweeps Old Oyster Bar." December 3, 1977.

————. "A French-Type Restaurant 'On Menu.'" April 27, 1963.

————. "Japanese Restaurant Due." December 26, 1964.

————. "New French Restaurant Atop '4 Seasons' Stresses Elegance." January 25, 1964.

————. "The Down Under Started." May 25, 1968.

Fort Lauderdale Sunday News. "'Flying Tigers' Unit Will Have Reunion." September 30, 1956.

Franke, Fred. "Prohibition Days Recalled. Had a Speakeasy." *Fort Lauderdale News*, September 27, 1968.

Freund, Bob. "Barbecued Baby Ribs Built Kim's Cabin." *Fort Lauderdale News*, September 15, 1964.

————. "New Restaurant, Seven Pillars Going Up on Sunrise." *Fort Lauderdale News and Sun-Sentinel*, November 18, 1962.

————. "Wenner Opens New Spot-Law School Bows to Food." *Fort Lauderdale News*, November 13, 1964.

Froman, Andrew. "Teaching Comes from the Heart." *Fort Lauderdale News*, June 11, 1980.

Greenbaum, Kurt. "Cars Bask for Last Time at Landmark Restaurant." *Sun-Sentinel*, September 29, 1986.

Hartz, Deborah S. "Soup-to-Nuts Primer for Chowderheads." *Orlando Sentinel*, February 18, 2004.

Hawks, Roy. "Pizio's Drive Inn Popular for Food Since 1939 Opening." *Post-Standard* (Syracuse, NY), September 8, 1961.

Hinton, Dave. "It's Four-Score Plus 1 for 'Mr. Restaurant.'" *Fort Lauderdale News*, July 5, 1960.

Hoder, Randye. "Landmark Lauderdale Restaurant Closes After 28 Years." *Fort Lauderdale News and Sun-Sentinel*, October 4, 1987.

————. "Restaurant Chain Eyes Bryan Homes." *Sun-Sentinel*, July 2, 1987.

————. "Setting Sale." *Fort Lauderdale News*, October 16, 1987.

Hoekstra, Dick. "Round Table's Hearth Offers Variety." *Fort Lauderdale News*, January 1962.

————. "Talented Kings IV Electrifies Bonanza Room Crowd." *Fort Lauderdale News and Sun-Sentinel*, October 1, 1961.

Hoffman, Ken. "Bachelors III: Old Faces, New Image." *Fort Lauderdale News and Sun-Sentinel*, November 11, 1978.

Hopkins, John. "Suzette, The Drunken Swine, Entertains Restaurant Patrons." *Fort Lauderdale Daily News*, June 3, 1950.

Jensen, Trevor. "Lucile Brewer, 81, Operated Eatery." *Sun-Sentinel*, November 22, 1991.

Jewish Post (Marion County, Indianapolis). "Left Indianapolis." January 9, 1976.

————. "Saul Hochman, 81, owned Sam's Subway." July 23, 2003.

Kelley, Lane. "Ernie's Restaurant Gets New Owner, Keeps Old Ambience." *Sun-Sentinel*, May 27, 1997.

LaMendola, Bob. "Charles Creighton, Restaurateur." *Sun-Sentinel*, March 1, 1991.

————. "R-Donuts Closure Strips Lauderdale of Another Custom." *Sun-Sentinel*, August 1, 1990.

Langberg, Mike. "Restaurateur Innovates as Times, Tastes, Change." *Fort Lauderdale News*, February 27, 1984.

Lassiter, Tom. "Winston Lee, Owned Local Restaurants." *Sun-Sentinel*, August 23, 1990.

Lynch, Ray. "Dorothy Heilman, Ran Family Eateries." *Sun-Sentinel*, March 7, 1990.

Mayo, Michael. "Bravo Ristorante Near Port Everglades Closes After 28 Years." *Sun-Sentinel*, June 17, 2019.

————. "Ernie's Bar-B-Q, Fort Lauderdale Mainstay for 60 Years, 'Officially Closed' after Sale." *Sun-Sentinel*, March 28, 2017.

————. "A 'Living Wake' for a Dying Bar." *Sun-Sentinel*, January 9, 2017.

————. "A Local Legend's Not Ready for Last Call." *Sun-Sentinel*, August 4, 2002.

————. "Mangos, Longtime Fixture on Las Olas Blvd., is Sold." *Sun-Sentinel*, January 31, 2017.

————. "Remembering Burt Reynolds and Burt & Jack's Restaurant in Fort Lauderdale." *Sun-Sentinel*, September 7, 2018.

Mummert, Patty. "Robbery Motive in Smalley Death." *Fort Lauderdale News*, January 9, 1967.

Nolin, Robert. "Popular Eatery Thrived, Then Fell Victim to Terrorists." *Sun-Sentinel*, March 18, 2015.

Rejtman, Jack. "Yesterday's Gone." *Miami Herald*, December 10, 1999.

Rich, Candace. "He Brings a Little Paris to Las Olas." *Fort Lauderdale News*, September 21, 1977.

Roberts, Elizabeth. "Moy Matriarch Turns 90." *Sun-Sentinel*, June 4, 2003.

Rubinkowski, Leslie. "Spice of Life." *Sun-Sentinel*, July 19, 1988.

Sallee, Anne. "A Trip Back into Porky's Heyday." *Oakland Park Gazette*, October 19, 2013.

Satchell, Arlene. "Chinese Restaurant Pioneer Moy Lee Dies at 92." *Sun-Sentinel*, February 28, 2012.

Schneider, Ben. "Sweden Houses OK by Yumping Yimmies." *Fort Lauderdale News and Sun-Sentinel*, July 4, 1971.

Segall, Grant. "Restaurateur-Turned-Poet Is Globetrotter for His Craft." *Fort Lauderdale News*, June 14, 1982.

Selinger, Hank. "Joe's: An Ode to Honest Food." *Miami Herald*, April 25, 1982.

Stein, Gary. "Waitress Serves Up Memories." *Fort Lauderdale News and Sun-Sentinel*, January 6, 1985.

Stratton, Jeff. "A House Surrounded." *Broward Palm Beach New Times*, February 7, 2002.

Sun-Sentinel. "City Link Restaurants, Café Blue Fish." March 30, 2010.

———. "Yesterday's Restaurant Goes Out of Business." April 23, 2004.

Tolf, Robert. "Cajun House Cooking Shines." *Fort Lauderdale News and Sun-Sentinel*, November 25, 1983.

———. "La Perla a Gem at a Moderate Price." *Fort Lauderdale News and Sun-Sentinel*, January 3, 1986.

———. "Long Distance Recommendation." *Fort Lauderdale News*, December 10, 1976.

———. "Maharaja Blazed a Trail, Is Still at the Forefront." *Fort Lauderdale News*, June 20, 1975.

———. "Pancho's Shows Promise." *Fort Lauderdale News and Sun-Sentinel*, May 10, 1985.

Valverde, Miriam. "Café de Paris to Close After 50 Years on Las Olas." *Sun-Sentinel*, May 5, 2016.

Walker, Meg. "Etson James Blackwell, 90, Managed Stranahan Restaurant." *Sun-Sentinel*, September 28, 1991.

Williams, Mary C. "V. Bi Leo, La Perla Co-Owner." *Sun-Sentinel*, May 12, 1994.

Zink, Jack. "Moy Lee's Promises to Become Popular." *Fort Lauderdale News*, January 31, 1975.

———. "Seventies Usher in New Era of Glittery, Top-Rank Talent for Night Life in Broward." *Fort Lauderdale News*, March 30, 1976.

Book

Barnette, Michael C. *Encyclopedia of Florida Shipwrecks.* Vol. 1, *Atlantic Coast.* St. Petersburg, FL: Association of Underwater Explorers, 2010.

Personal Interviews

Blaikie, Sandra Chichester. Personal interview with the author, May 28, 2019.
Burlingame, Cindy Sowers. Personal interview with the author, May 30, 2019.
Day, John. Personal interview with the author, May 22, 2019.
House, Darrell. Personal interview with the author, May 22, 2019.
Jackson, Jack. Personal interview with the author, May 23, 2019.
Koch, Mike. Personal interview with the author, May 28, 2019.
Middlebrooks, Dean. Personal interview with the author, May 22, 2019.
Pizio, Ted. Personal interview with the author, May 31, 2019.
Ramsden, Clint. Personal interview with the author, May 30, 2019.
Samp, Butch. Personal interview with the author, May 27, 2019.
Watson, Scott. Personal interview with the author, May 29, 2019.
Willis, Ginger. Personal interview with the author, Nov 13, 1997.
Zimmerman, Lawrence "Zero." Personal interview with the author, May 26, 2019.

Websites

Facebook. "Bravo Ristorante." www.facebook.com.
Facebook. "Ernie's BBQ and Lounge." www.facebook.com.
Facebook. "I Grew Up in South Florida in the 60's, 70's and 80's." www.facebook.com.
Facebook. "Sea Grill Restaurant in Ft. Lauderdale, FL." www.facebook.com.
Facebook. "South Florida The Way We Remember It." www.facebook.com.
Facebook. "You Know You're from Fort Lauderdale If…." www.facebook.com.
Goreil, Leila. "Cornerstone Vacation Ownership Continues U.S. Expansion with New Headquarters in Florida." www.cornerstonevo.com.
My Florida History. "Sweden House Smorgasbord." www.myfloridahistory.blogspot.com.
South Florida Diving Headquarters. "Ancient Mariner." www.southfloridadiving.com.
TripAdvisor. "Le Café de Paris." www.tripadvisor.com.
Tumblr. "F Troop Trio." www.oldshowbiz.tumblr.com.
Whitaker, Jan. "Roast Beef Frenzy." www.restaurant-ingthroughhistory.com.
Yelp. "Maguire's Hill 16." www.yelp.com.
Yelp. "Old Florida Seafood House." www.yelp.com.

Index

L

M

Y

Z

About the Authors

A native Iowan, TODD BOTHEL has lived in Fort Lauderdale since 2003. He holds a bachelor's degree in anthropology from Beloit College (Wisconsin) and a master's degree in museum studies from John F. Kennedy University (California). An avid historian, Todd has worked in the museum field for nearly twenty-five years, researching and installing exhibits covering a wide variety of subjects. He currently works at the Jewish Museum of Florida-FIU in Miami Beach. This is Todd's fourth book exploring the history of Fort Lauderdale. He has also conducted research for eight other books and exhibition catalogs.

"TRAPPER" DAN SANTORO first visited Fort Lauderdale Beach during spring break in 1979, and he returned each of the following two years. He permanently moved to "Fort Liquordale" in 1986 and quickly immersed himself in the hospitality scene there, working and making friends with dozens of like-minded individuals and vacationers while soaking up the sun and the history of the city.

After the death of the godfather of spring break, "Crazy Gregg" Newell, in 2003, Dan was dared by his friends to write the ultimate history of one of America's hottest destinations, and *Where the Boys (and Girls) Were!* met that challenge head on. You are welcome to contact him for more information on the history of Fort Lauderdale Beach by visiting his website, *www.fortlauderdalebeachbook.com*.

Visit us at
www.historypress.com